PREFACE

❏ DEAR FRIENDS,

■ Whether you are new to mediation or an experienced mediator looking for new perspectives on your work, we hope this *Mediator's Handbook* will be an ongoing resource for you.

■ The field of mediation has expanded dramatically since Friends Conflict Resolution Programs (FCRP) put together the first *Handbook* in 1982. From a little-known concept developed by community activists on the one hand and by the courts on the other, mediation processes have spread throughout the United States to communities, corporations, criminal justice systems, and government agencies. Mediation has become a profession, with university degrees and professional societies.

It has been amazing to watch this small experiment in alternative approaches to conflict become part of the everyday landscape. Although professional mediators provide a valuable role, FCRP remains convinced that many people can learn to use basic mediation processes and skills. Spreading this knowledge widely gives more people a positive, practical, and collaborative way to ease tense situations and to help others resolve their pressing concerns.

■ The model we present here is simple, yet it rests on a raft of skills that can take a long time to learn. The first section of the *Handbook* gives an overview of mediation and conflict. The second section, nicknamed "The Anatomy," lays out each step in the mediation process. The three Toolbox sections which follow detail the skills and approaches needed for the three main mediator tasks: Supporting the People, Controlling the Process, and Solving the Problem. The last section looks at informal mediation. The book is designed as a resource so that you can concentrate on areas that are relevant for you, explore new strategies, or prepare for an upcoming mediation.

■ The original *Handbook* was, we believe, the first "how-to" mediation manual available to the public. Copies have since surfaced in such far-removed places as South Africa, Costa Rica, Norway, Australia, Israel, Romania, and Burma. Mediators have found the FCRP model useful for working within corporations and institutions, for public policy and environmental issues, for family and community disputes, for schools, and in their private lives.

We offer this new edition to all the peacemakers around the world who are helping people find their own constructive solutions to the difficulties in their lives.

Cataloging in Publication Data:
A catalog record for this publication is available from the National Library of Canada.

First printing and copyright January 1982. Revised January 1984; April 1987.
Second edition May 1990.
Third edition August 1994; revised February 1996; February 1997.

Book design and layout by Jennifer Beer. Cover art by Karen Kerney.

Printed in Canada.
Sixteenth printing July 2010.

Paperback ISBN: 978-0-86571-359-8

To order directly from the publishers, please call toll-free (North America) 1-800-567-6772, or order online at www.newsociety.com

Any other inquiries can be directed by mail to:
New Society Publishers
P.O. Box 189, Gabriola Island, BC VOR IXO, Canada
1-250-247-9737

New Society Publishers' mission is to publish books that contribute in fundamental ways to building an ecologically sustainable and just society, and to do so with the least possible impact on the environment, in a manner that models this vision. We are committed to doing this not just through education, but through action. We are acting on our commitment to the world's remaining ancient forests by phasing out our paper supply from ancient forests worldwide. This book is one step toward ending global deforestation and climate change. It is printed on acid-free paper that is 100% old growth forest-free (100% post-consumer recycled), processed chlorine free, and printed with vegetable-based, low-VOC inks. For further information, or to browse our full list of books and purchase securely, visit our website at: www.newsociety.com

NEW SOCIETY PUBLISHERS   www.newsociety.com

CONTENTS

CONTRIBUTORS

❑ APPRECIATING OUR CONTRIBUTORS

The Mediator's Handbook is a collaborative project which, like a soup simmering on the back of the stove, owes its rich flavor to many cooks, not just to the handfuls of spice and fresh vegetables thrown in shortly before serving.

Friends Conflict Resolution Programs has been leading mediation trainings for twenty years, and the Handbook has evolved along with the program's accumulated experiences. Successive staff have added their perspectives and creativity to its pages, while mediators and trainees have helped clarify our thinking along the way.

Eileen Stief began FCRP's mediation program in 1976, along with Elisabeth Leonard and Emily Sontag. They developed FCRP's basic mediation process by trial and error, taking on disputes and experimenting with how to facilitate them successfully. In 1982, intern Jenny Beer put together their training materials into the first Handbook, guided by the wisdom and wit of staff member Charles Walker, who helped ground our mediation practice in Quaker principles.

In 1986, the program moved to downtown Philadelphia and the new generation of staff, Sandi Adams and Chel Avery, brought fresh commitment and intellectual vigor to FCRP's mediation work. They also expanded the training and upgraded the Handbook. Both of them have advised us on the revisions for this new edition. We are particularly indebted to Chel for the sections on cultural differences, interests, and when to intervene.

Today's staff, Keelin Barry and Caroline Packard, get special thanks, as they have been most patient in assisting with the long process of getting the new edition of the Handbook ready. They have gamely tried out the new sections in their training sessions and mediations. Caroline persuaded us to add "Setting the Agenda" to the mediation anatomy, and also helped us rethink the Exchange phase and aspects of understanding interests and issues.

In addition to FCRP staff, past and present, we particularly thank those who contributed their good thinking, editing, and proofing skills: Hans Dietze, Michael Doyle, Steve Moss, Michael Pan, Anne Richan, and Carol Fawcett Smith. Our illustrators, Elizabeth Elwood, Molly Haines, Jay Miller, and Jennifer Beer, helped liven the pages.

CONTRIBUTORS

Our sources of support and guidance:

For helping us publish this and past editions, Friends Conflict Resolution Programs thanks:

➤ The Bequests Committee of Philadelphia Yearly Meeting

➤ The Rice Family Foundation

➤ The Thomas H. & Mary Williams Shoemaker Fund

➤ Philadelphia Yearly Meeting for financial and office support.

We thank Chris Plant of New Society Publishers for bringing FCRP's work to a wider public. We appreciated his patience when technical difficulties in printing the *Handbook* seemed insurmountable, and his willingness to work collaboratively on book content and design despite those pressures.

The many Yearly Meeting members who have served on the FCRP and Friends Suburban Project committees have offered hands-on support and faithful guidance over an adventurous two decades. Nearly everyone who has been part of FCRP as staff, committee member, or community mediation program staff has continued to mediate and train for FCRP and for other groups. We like what we do! And we hope that the collective knowledge gathered in this *Handbook*—our long-simmering pot of soup—will have lasting value for our readers as well.

OVERVIEW

❑ WHAT IS MEDIATION?

Mediation is any process for resolving disputes in which another person helps the parties negotiate a settlement.

In one sense, mediation is no big deal. People have been mediating for as long as people have been fighting and most of us pick up mediation skills from our everyday experiences. In another sense, mediation as a *formal* process has only recently become commonplace outside of labor and international disputes. In North America, using mediation for personal, organizational, and public conflicts is still a fledgling idea. This handbook presents a structured mediation process which is designed for resolving these conflicts which arise in our work, our communities, and our relationships.

❑ DOES IT REALLY HELP?

Mediation is useful in a wide variety of conflicts, particularly in the *aftermath* of an incident, at the point when emotions have eased enough that the parties can begin to negotiate.

Mediation can sometimes work spectacularly well. The participants resolve problems, let go their sense of grievance, and mend broken relationships. Occasionally, mediation sessions crash and burn, leaving parties feeling more angry and hopeless than before. Usually, the outcome is less dramatic: people find answers to at least some of their concerns and walk away emotionally relieved, with an agreement that they will for the most part uphold.

How does a two-hour mediation session create a turning point in conflicts that have sometimes festered for years? Mediation gives people the chance to air their wounds. Intense conflict tends to generate misunderstanding and suspicion; many of these evaporate when the parties are able to talk directly. Because mediation is not bound by the rules of a formal proceeding, the parties can bring up whatever concerns them most—they are not restricted to those issues which are the official, public subject of dispute. Finally, the written agreement helps: even if a mediated agreement does not end a conflict, it can protect the parties from further friction and misunderstandings so that the conflict can fade away.

Success lies partly in the mediators' skills, but also with the readiness of the parties. If someone is bent on keeping a conflict going, even the most obvious solutions will not work. If everyone wants to see a conflict end, mediation can be a graceful and efficient way to do so.

THE MEDIATION PROCESS

❑ THE PROCESS

Mediators often speak reverently about "trusting the process." They tell stories about mediations where the parties seemed bitterly entrenched; yet by the second hour, those same stubborn, angry people were engaged in a friendly, productive discussion.

Let's look first at the rather simple "anatomy" of that process, the core pattern of the structured mediation sessions presented in this handbook. Note that Separate Meetings "float" rather than being locked into the sequence; mediators insert them whenever needed.

THE ANATOMY OF A MEDIATION SESSION

1. **Opening Statement**

2. **Uninterrupted Time**

3. **The Exchange**

4. **Setting the Agenda**

5. **Building the Agreement**

6. **Writing the Agreement**

7. **Closing Statement**

Separate Meetings

1. Opening Statement

Mediations are held in a neutral place at a time convenient to the parties. Sessions last approximately two hours.

The mediators—two are usually preferable to one—open the session with a welcome and an explanation of what will happen.

2. Uninterrupted Time

Each person takes a turn speaking while everyone else listens. For the most part, this is open-ended: the person can talk briefly or at length about anything relevant to the situation.

3. The Exchange

Then the arguing and discussion begin. For a while people accuse each other and attempt to set each other straight on the facts. They explain why they are upset; they make demands.

The mediators keep the discussion in bounds, making sure that each person is heard and each is protected. The mediators do not try to determine the truth or who is at fault. Rather, they listen for what matters to people and for possible areas of agreement. Sometimes, the Exchange brings about what we call a "turning point" of reconciliation.

... Separate Meetings

Separate Meetings can occur any time during the mediation and have many uses: checking out a person's concerns, confronting unhelpful behavior, or helping people think through their options.

4. Setting the Agenda

Discussion shifts towards the future: what will happen from now on? The parties agree on an agenda of issues which need resolution.

5. Building the Agreement

The parties work through each issue on the agenda, generating a number of ideas, then weighing, adjusting, and testing the alternatives to craft a workable, mutually satisfactory solution.

6 & 7. Writing the Agreement & Closing

If the parties are able to settle their differences, the mediators write a formal agreement containing those decisions. Everyone present signs and takes a copy home. The mediators review what has been accomplished, remind people of next steps, and wish them well.

THE MEDIATION PROCESS

❑ FCRP MEDIATION PROCESS: DISTINCTIVE CHARACTERISTICS

The practice and philosophy of mediation differs significantly from program to program and mediator to mediator. Here are some of the characteristics of Friends Conflict Resolution Programs' mediation process:

1. Who is present

Voluntary participation. Even though parties are often pressured to attend, the mediator stresses that they can still choose not to participate, and that the agreement will only contain things that all parties have genuinely agreed to.

Variety of mediators. Anyone can learn to use this mediation process. Formal mediators do not need higher education degrees, but they do need substantive training and apprenticeship. Mediators in specialized areas such as divorce, labor, multi-party, or international arenas need additional professional training.

No representatives. Lawyers are not present but may advise clients between sessions or before an agreement is finalized. Each member of a party is encouraged to speak for themselves.

Co-mediators. Mediators work in pairs, rather than solo or on panels.

2. Basic Structure

Flexible process. Mediators follow the basic anatomy of a mediation session, but do not work from a script.

Two hour sessions. Full sessions last 1½ to 2½ hours. Most situations are resolved in one or two sessions.

Separate Meetings when needed. The mediators can call a Separate Meeting whenever it seems appropriate. Some mediations have no Separate Meetings. The purpose is usually to help the parties negotiate better, not to provide shuttle diplomacy.

Informal tone. Mediators strive for a relatively informal, conversational tone, casting themselves as facilitators rather than as authority figures.

3. Purpose & Focus

Looking at the wider picture. Parties discuss the general situation, not just their immediate complaints. Anyone may raise issues which are not part of the official problem that brought them to mediation.

Airing Emotions. Expressing strong emotion is appropriate as long as it is not an attack; however, venting emotion is not the focus or goal.

The solutions are theirs. Parties do the hard work of speaking for themselves and working out mutually acceptable solutions. Mediators do not craft solutions for the parties.

Success is more than problem-solving. The goal of mediation is to help people improve their future relations and gain confidence in handling conflicts. Problem-solving is important, but reaching a detailed agreement is not the sole or ultimate measure of success.

Valuing reconciliation. Although most parties do not leave a mediation as good friends, nor do mediators press parties to reconcile, we hope that at the least they come to a greater understanding of and empathy for the other parties' point of view.

WHEN DOES MEDIATION WORK?

Mediation is most likely to resolve a conflict when:

➢ The parties want a resolution, or at least a change.

➢ All the important stakeholders come to the table.

➢ The parties are (eventually) able to express the reasons for their discomfort and distress.

➢ The mediator is able to control and sustain the process.

➢ The parties are capable of living up to their promises.

GUIDING PRINCIPLES

Friends Conflict Resolution Programs is committed to mediation which respects all who participate and provides nonviolent alternatives for resolving difficult conflicts. We believe that the most satisfying and lasting resolutions come about when every person takes part and agrees to the outcome.

❏ NONVIOLENT ALTERNATIVES

There are many ways to try to resolve a dispute: avoiding, ignoring, threatening, quitting, going to court, negotiating, hiring a lawyer, protesting, calling the police, filing a grievance, getting even, or going to arbitration. Asking a third party to mediate is yet another alternative.

Because mediation is based on respect for all participants, it seeks to diminish the influence of threats and fear and find solutions that are in everyone's interest. This process can help turn parties away from more coercive or even violent actions.

❏ CONSENSUS

Our mediation model grew out of Quaker process for finding the "sense of the meeting," where the group as a whole tries to discern the right action to take. Instead of choosing between various proposals, the group's decision emerges from a process of collective deliberation. Each person can have a substantive say in the group's decision.

Quaker process is rooted in worship and the search for truth, while the mediation process is secular. Nevertheless, they share these common elements:

> **Personal experience.** The seeds of resolution are within the situation and within the parties themselves. Discussion is grounded in personal experience, especially inward experience. The group as a whole weighs and integrates those individual perspectives.

> **Emergent resolutions.** Decisions will not be a simple compromise but will emerge, sometimes in surprising new forms, from the knowledge, deliberation, and creativity of all present.

> **Unity.** The resolution should address the most important concerns of all present even though it may not be 100% satisfying to any one person. If anyone is uneasy with the proposal, the majority does not override that person, but continues to search for a mutually satisfactory resolution.

The group collectively seeks to generate multiple alternatives and find a path that all participants can follow. Facilitators try to highlight areas of common agreement, at the same time making sure that difficult issues get attention. Consensus process therefore differs from other kinds of democratic methods such as voting, debate, the politics of compromise, forming alliances, or parliamentary procedure.

At its best, this kind of inclusive process, while at times frustratingly slow, can transform the parties and the conflict, and produce solutions which are not just workable but feel right to all involved.

❑ RESPECT

The guiding principle is respect for the disputants …

Mediation's consensus process assumes that dignity and participation are more important than efficiency and expertise. It rests on the expectation that:

➢ Every person has an element of goodwill and integrity

➢ Every person is capable of change

➢ People can and should make decisions about their own lives

➢ The parties speak for themselves, think for themselves, decide for themselves. The hard work is theirs. So is the outcome.

This mediation process was designed to strengthen the ability of individuals, organizations, and communities to handle their own conflicts. The mediator provides a structure for parties to increase honest communication, air emotions, and solve problems. In effect, mediation gives angry people a chance to bring out the best in themselves.

… and for the ability of many different people to mediate effectively.

We are also committed to spreading basic mediation skills; these are life skills, not just esoteric techniques for professionals. Anyone can learn to use the process and the skills described in this handbook.

UNDERSTANDING CONFLICT

❑ UNDERSTANDING CONFLICT

How you understand conflict will guide the way you mediate. This section outlines the perspectives on conflict which underlie the mediation approach described in this handbook.

Life is full of annoyances, opposing interests, cultural differences, dislikes, insults, differences of opinion, and divergent interpretations. Only a fraction of those grow into a pattern of hostilities—those more serious, ongoing situations that we define as "conflicts." (A "dispute" is a particular incident, a visible piece of the larger conflict.)

The next three pages map out some different characteristics of conflict: the sense of threat which drives it, what happens when it escalates, and the three primary aspects of conflict that a mediation process needs to address.

❑ THE CONFLICT CORE

The Conflict Core diagram shows the sense of threat that pulses at the core of most conflicts. This is not to say that a few people don't leap into conflicts for the sheer pleasure of turmoil or opportunity for gain. Or one party may be heavily invested in the conflict while the other shows little anxiety or interest—perhaps because their own core concerns are not threatened or they have the upper hand. By the time they get to the table, the parties are usually feeling under siege. Something important is at stake, they are suspicious and afraid, and this keeps them from resolving the dispute.

From a mediator's point of view, many disputes seem irrational or trivial. Why are these people fighting about this? For whatever reason, this particular situation touches these people in deep and painful ways. If the threat is powerful enough, they may act—heroically, foolishly, or meanly—in exaggerated ways they would never do otherwise. People do not expend such intense life energy on something that doesn't matter to them, even if from the outside it is hard to understand what motivates the person to do so.

Mediation can alleviate that sense of threat. The parties can hear directly from the other side instead of relying on rumor and interpretation. Also, a written agreement can offer a measure of security. Freed from that anxiety, the participants have the opportunity to think more productively and honestly about their conflict, act on that wider perspective, and eventually they may be able to turn their attention to other things.

THE CONFLICT CORE

Conflict emerges when
disagreements, differences, annoyances,
competition, or inequities
threaten something important.

Their lies could ruin
my good reputation.

This is humiliating.

I might lose my job.

I want my privacy.

I deserve respect.

I might be attacked.

Annoyance

Disagreement

She thinks I'm stupid.

I can't meet my
basic needs.

Inequities

Competition

My kids could get hurt.

I've been shut out.

No one will listen to me
after this.

This will bankrupt me.

I won't be the expert
any longer.

I hate feeling
intimidated.

He might kill me.

I'm losing control of this
department.

UNDERSTANDING CONFLICT

❑ THE CONFLICT SPIRAL

As conflict intensifies, all kinds of consequences spiral outward, affecting individuals, relationships, tasks and decisions, and sometimes whole organizations and communities.

Personal responses. The stress of conflict provokes strong feelings of anxiety, anger, hostility, depression, and even vengeance. Every action or non-action of the other side becomes suspect. People become increasingly rigid in how they see the problem and what solutions they demand. It can be difficult for them to think clearly or to see what is happening.

Community responses. When the dispute begins to affect those around it, people may take sides or leave. Organizations bend or invent new rules and structures to contain the situation.

Politicization. At some point, the dispute becomes public. Authorities are drawn in. Each side develops set positions and gathers allies for the cause. At this point the conflict may spread beyond the original protagonists' control.

The conflict spiral on the next page illustrates the many elements of an expanding conflict. Beneath what seems from the outside to be a few resolvable issues is a dense, interconnected web of connections and consequences which is difficult to unsnarl. Small wonder disputants feel discouraged by the time they get to mediation.

❑ THE CONFLICT TRIANGLE: PEOPLE, PROCESS, AND PROBLEMS

The Conflict Triangle on the following page sorts the spiral elements into three categories. These give mediators a basic framework for assessing the conflict.

➢ **People.** Every conflict involves a history of relationships and personalities.

➢ **Process.** People fight in different ways, but every conflict has patterns of interaction: the ways it intensifies, eases, or spreads.

➢ **Problem.** And finally, every conflict has content—the issues and interests that are the "reason" for the dispute.

Any lasting resolution must recognize all three sides of the conflict. This triangle is an organizing theme throughout the *Handbook*, because each side of the conflict triangle demands its own set of mediation skills and its own rationale.

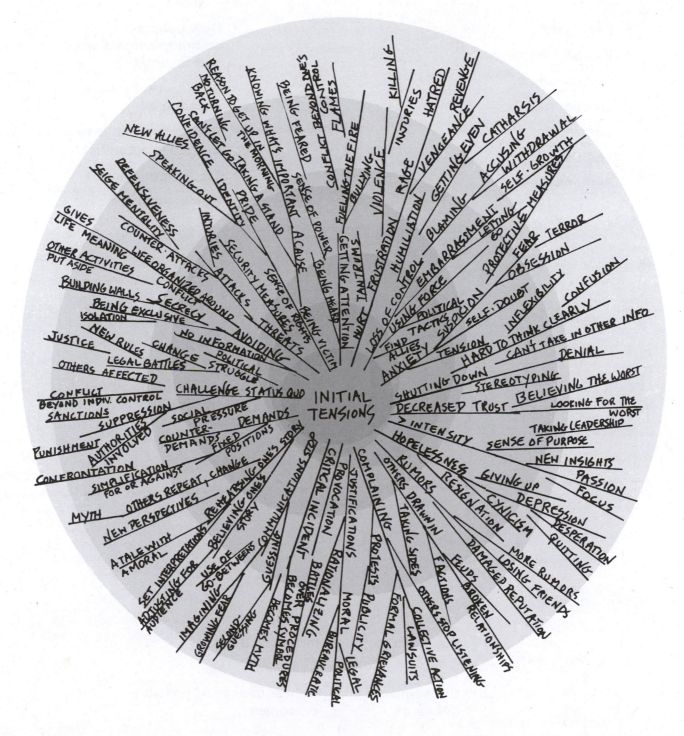

THE CONFLICT TRIANGLE

- Past history
- Values, meanings
- Relationships
- Emotions
- Behavior
- Abilities
- Personalities

- How people communicate issues and feelings
- Structures, systems, procedures
- Norms about how to behave in a conflict
- Decision-making
- Roles, jobs

PEOPLE

PROCESS

PROBLEM

- Facts
- Positions
- Issues
- Consequences of events

- Perceptions
- Interests, Needs
- Solutions
- Consequences of possible outcomes

TRANSFORMING CONFLICT

❑ RECOGNIZING THE OTHER

Reconciliation goes a step beyond plain resolution of a conflict. It is born when one party recognizes that the other is a real person with feelings, needs, rights, pains, hopes.

As histories and passions build up in the conflict spiral, people construct high walls to keep pain—and therefore other perspectives—out. The ideal moment for mediation is when the parties find themselves boxed in by those walls, tired of how things are, yet uncertain about how to open up communication without tearing down the wall that protects them.

Some parties in a mediation have lower barriers; they actively seek to communicate and understand. These people are a mediator's joy. At the other end of the spectrum are people who are so invested in their own miseries, so certain of their own view of the world, that no amount of listening or speaking seems to register in their consciousness.

The structure of the mediation can create a zone for people to tentatively let down their guard; the mediators' presence and the mediation process substitutes for the protective wall.

❑ TRANSFORMING CONFLICT

It is in this sense that mediation at its best goes beyond problem-solving or "managing" a conflict. If the participants are able to address each side of the conflict triangle, easing their emotional state, changing their ways of interacting, and fixing the problems which threatened their core interests, then the conflict is not merely resolved: mindsets and hearts change. The whole situation shifts.

Not many mediations bring about such noticeable transformation, yet every so often a mediator has the privilege of providing the setting for such transformation. We keep open that possibility when we sit down at the table—just in case the moment is right.

WHEN IS MEDIATION USEFUL?

❑ WHEN IS MEDIATION USEFUL?

If several of these are true, a mediation may be effective:

✓ The issues are complicated by a strong emotional element.

✓ The parties know each other.

✓ Maintaining a relationship with the other party is important.

✓ One party feels uncomfortable confronting the other side unless someone else is present.

✓ The parties work or live together, or for other reasons cannot avoid the conflict.

✓ A decision must be reached soon.

✓ The parties doubt their own ability to work out the problem.

✓ Many people are involved or indirectly affected.

✓ One or both parties want to avoid formal proceedings.

❑ WHEN IS MEDIATION NOT APPROPRIATE?

Mediation may be unsuccessful or even harmful. Do not recommend mediation if *any* of the following are true:

✓ A serious incident has just occurred and people are still too upset to carry on a useful conversation.

✓ You strongly suspect one party intends to use the mediation to escalate the dispute (to threaten, to gather information, to look good in front of the judge, etc.).

✓ One party seems incapable of listening to anything you say, or seems otherwise too disturbed to negotiate a workable agreement.

✓ The main problem is, in your judgment, unmediatable.

✓ You believe that one party might be better off using the courts or other forum. Power imbalance makes fair agreement unlikely.

✓ The issue deserves public attention so that mediation does not hide a problem or a settlement from public knowledge (e.g. concealing environmental or work dangers; racial harassment patterns).

✓ Key parties are unwilling to participate.

WHEN IS MEDIATION USEFUL?

❑ WHAT DISPUTES CAN BE MEDIATED?

The sample situations on the following pages illustrate the wide variety of settings where basic mediation can be effective. The examples range from home with family and friends, to the community, the workplace, the marketplace, and large institutions.

In some ways, the *kind of resolution* the parties desire is a better gauge of whether mediation is feasible than the *content* of the dispute. For instance, disputing parties may be concerned about larger issues of justice and prefer to press for a public or legal forum to air a situation. Others may care more about being publicly vindicated or getting revenge than about preventing future troubles. Still others may judge that they will win using their current strategies or lose if they have to negotiate.

Conversely, if the parties are ready to talk and to make changes, mediation can successfully help resolve many substantively different kinds of longstanding, complex, and bitter conflicts.

❑ SPECIALIZED MEDIATION

Other types of disputes require specialized training to mediate and are not reviewed here. Nevertheless, we note that the basic process described in this Handbook has proved remarkably flexible, and will give you a sturdy foundation for learning to mediate in these more complex arenas.

Public and institutional disputes

➢ Public interest multi-party disputes involving constituencies, such as the siting of a waste dump or the widening of a highway.

➢ Labor-management negotiations and grievance proceedings.

➢ Organizational and workplace disputes, both internal (between individuals, between departments, within boards and teams) and between organizations (for example partnerships or headquarter/subsidiary tensions).

➢ Difficulties with public agencies or with compliance: for example, disputes involving EEOC (equal employment), disabilities and other non-discrimination acts, or the delivery of special education services.

WHEN IS MEDIATION USEFUL?

Following up hot conflicts or crime

➢ Victims meeting with offenders.

➢ Mediations which follow incidents of violence, or hot conflict.

➢ Multinational or ethnic disputes.

➢ Mediations which occur during a protracted war or conflict, at the formal diplomatic level, the backstage informal level, or with civilians and activists at the grassroots level.

Disputes involving families, children

➢ Divorce, custody, and post-divorce mediation to help parents make decisions about their children.

➢ Family situations which also involve therapy.

➢ School peer mediation, special education parent-school mediation

Consumer disputes

➢ Disputes between businesses and customers.

➢ Difficulties between institutions and their clients, such as patient care insurance coverage issues or student grievances at a university.

❑ SAMPLE SITUATIONS

Non-Profit Organizations

■ The board of GoodWorks is split between its visionary founder and its business-oriented new executive. A mediator who was hired to assess the situation recommended a private mediation with the executive, the founder, and one other long-time board member, to be followed by a facilitated "clearing the air" session with the whole board.

■ A Narcotics Anonymous group has met at the Community Center for four years and has been arguing with the staff for the past two. Representatives from each have agreed to sit down and discuss several thorny issues: unpaid fees, the Center's upkeep of facilities, scheduling problems, littering, and innuendoes that NA types of people are not wanted at the Center.

Consumer

■ The Stones have refused to pay Frank Davies, a local carpenter, until he refinishes a door and several cupboards. This work was not part of the written contract, but the Stones claim Davies agreed to do these side jobs. Davies called the local mediation service.

■ A public hospital has trouble getting patients to pay. With a mediator they work out a streamlined agreement form for incoming patients, and a process, which may or may not involve the mediator, to meet with patients to work out a realistic payment schedule.

Neighbors

■ The Schiffleys and the Klopps have both filed complaints against each other claiming harassment. They share a common driveway and have fought about cars, loud music, and torn-up lawns for six years. The Klopps' valuable chestnut tree shades the Shiffleys' garden. The magistrate referred them to dispute resolution.

■ Wilma, 73 and living alone, complains that Tim, Paul, and Chester, neighboring 12-year-olds, have been harassing her. Lately, the parents have also become involved. Accusations include a vandalized garden, some confiscated frisbees, and late-night phone calls. A senior citizen center arranged the mediation.

SAMPLE SITUATIONS

Landlord / Tenant

■ The lease permits animals but the landlady, Mrs. DiGiovanni, insists that Parker get rid of his cat. Neighboring apartments have complained that his cat is left for hours in the hall without food and smells up the building. Parker claims that DiGiovanni is harassing him for racial reasons. He has a long-term lease with a mediation clause.

■ Victor moved out of Garden View Apartments because he couldn't afford the rent. He has been looking for work for six months. The landlord found damages exceeding the initial deposit. Victor admits to some of the damage but has no money to pay for them. The landlord called the city's mediation program because he doubted that going to court would help recover the money.

Family and Friends

■ Mike, 16, ran off to stay with a friend after a raging argument with his father. The father is angry about Mike's language and lack of a job, while Mike is outraged that his father won't allow him to play sports after school. Mike's mother insists that Mike come home. He refuses, but agrees to come to a mediation.

■ Martha and Alice were good friends who were active in a local theater company. However, arguments about some items that were loaned and accusations of betraying confidences have resulted in a bitter break. Martha has dropped out of a production 3 weeks before show time so she won't have to see Alice. Members of the company have pressed them into mediating the situation.

■ Henry is increasingly forgetful and frail. After months of acrimony and denial, his three children and several grandchildren and Henry are meeting with a mediator to work out an agreement detailing who should handle Henry's money, who will find him an appropriate nursing home, and who will clean out and sell the house.

SAMPLE SITUATIONS

Schools and Colleges

■ Harry and Cliff are roommates. They are quarreling about sleeping hours, laptop "borrowing", and smelly laundry strewn around the room. Harry complains that Cliff's girlfriend is always there and he has no privacy. The resident advisor recommended mediation.

■ Althea and Sheila had a major fight during Art class and both were suspended. Althea claims that Sheila smashed her sculpture on purpose. Althea pushed Sheila on the stairway. The school is afraid that their friends will make the feud worse. Althea and Sheila were asked to meet with student mediators to talk things over before coming back to school.

■ Xian has complained to the University about a teaching assistant's punitive grading and rude treatment after he challenged the TA in class. The professor was unable to determine what had really happened and suggested the TA ask the campus ombuds office to mediate.

Congregations

■ Tensions came to a head during the last Building and Grounds Committee meeting when Barbara walked out. Most members are friends of Arthur, who believes that the congregation should care for the property themselves in order to save money. Barbara has had many arguments with Arthur over slipshod maintenance and wants to hire a caretaker. She is furious with his condescending, autocratic manner; he says she is a whining airhead. The whole committee is meeting with a mediator.

■ Representatives of a church congregation are meeting with neighbors to discuss neighborhood complaints: noise, parking in front of their houses, and a political banner about abortion on the church lawn. The neighborhood leader asked a mediator to facilitate the meeting.

SAMPLE SITUATIONS

Small business

■ Sydney manages a craft shop. He has told the owner, Teresa, that he will quit unless she fires her niece Myra, who works there on weekends. Teresa has talked to both Sydney and Myra separately and established that Myra's competence is not an issue; the two just have very different styles and irritate each other easily. Teresa has asked Sydney and Myra to meet with a mediator before she makes a decision.

■ Electrician Gerry thought he had a good personal relationship with the owner of Tom's Toy Store. However, Tom's Toys is now four months behind in paying for a major rewiring job he did for them. The owner won't return his calls. Gerry would like to get his money without having to take Tom's Toys to court. When the mediator talks to Tom's Toys, she finds out that the store is withholding payment because the job was not done to their specifications.

Corporations and bureaucracies

■ Two managers from a manufacturing department came to the company ombuds office, which offers confidential advising, mediation, and advocacy services to anyone in the company. They had approached a marketing manager to discuss a long list of complaints about the poor coordination between their departments. However, the marketing manager said he had no time to talk with such incompetent people, and walked out. The ombuds person met with the marketing manager several times before persuading him that it was in his best interest to have a confidential meeting with the manufacturing managers before this mess hit the vice president's desk.

■ Three secretaries who share one large office communicate through curt notes because they are no longer speaking to each other. Nicole, their supervisor, has no cause to fire any of them and has tried various strategies to get them to work together better. But whatever the problem is, they aren't willing to discuss it with her or each other. Last week, Nicole ordered them to sit down with someone trained in mediation from Personnel and deal with it.

❏ WHO MAKES A GOOD MEDIATOR?

Different communities and different types of disputes need different mediators. There is much room for varied personalities and experience. However, some personal characteristics and skills are particularly valuable in mediation.

➢ Strong "people skills," especially giving good attention.

➢ Able to be directive and to confront.

➢ Comfortable with high emotion, arguments, interruptions, tears.

➢ Respected and trusted.

➢ Imaginative in solving problems.

➢ Patient as disputants inch their way towards resolution.

➢ Able to empathize and be gentle, to withhold judgment.

➢ Impartial: putting aside one's own opinions, reactions, and even some principles.

➢ Low need for recognition, credit, having things turn out your way.

❏ THE SATISFACTIONS OF MEDIATING

FCRP mediators speak about the challenges and satisfactions of mediating:

People get discouraged… You have doubts too, but it is important to say, "Yes, you are getting somewhere. You are talking." It is a miracle to see at the end of the session how it has come together.

The simplicity of it is almost embarrassing. In two hours people can solve "impossible" problems and let out hostility which has sometimes built up for years. The exciting part of mediating is watching that process work again and again for different people in different situations.

I don't think I have ever done a mediation which hasn't in some way connected with my own experiences. Each time I help another person solve a problem, I do the same for my own life.

There is always a feeling of exhilaration when things work out. I almost always find some good thing about each disputant by the end.

Several weeks ago, an old woman and a young mother cried while they hugged each other at the end of a mediation.

I don't get as excited by a successful agreement as I used to, but their relief was so great, as if boulders they'd been carrying had just rolled away.

On my way home, I found myself getting teary just thinking about it.

—a community mediator

THE MEDIATOR

❏ CAN I MEDIATE?

Once you learn the basic mediation format and hone the people, process, and problem-solving skills found in this book, you'll probably find yourself using them often. However, if you want to go the next step and mediate disputes in your community, on your job, or as a professional mediator, you will of course need good training (see page 166), an apprenticeship, and in some cases, official certification.

❏ ADVANTAGES OF CO-MEDIATION

When you are intervening in conflicts, the old proverb is usually right: two heads are better than one.

➢ A co-mediator can help you think more clearly each step of the way. The other mediator can be a support when you are uncertain how to proceed or when you find the disputants difficult or unpleasant.

➢ Because each mediator has a different personality and approach, co-mediation gives greater flexibility in responding to the parties and to different circumstances.

➢ Mediators can be selected for complementary experience, skills, or knowledge. When differences in race, gender, generation, class, or culture is an issue in a dispute, choosing mediators who are members of those groups helps disputants trust that the mediators can understand their situation.

➢ Having more than one mediator allows for dividing tasks: one facilitates while one writes up points of agreement; one follows a disputant who is leaving while the other stays at the table; one gives extra attention to a troubled disputant during the discussion; or one directs a hot discussion while the other takes thorough notes.

➢ You can learn different approaches by observing how other mediators handle the session.

➢ You have the opportunity to receive immediate feedback from other mediators.

➢ Working in pairs models collaboration for the parties.

THE MEDIATION SESSION

Preparation

Opening Statement

Uninterrupted Time

The Exchange

Separate Meetings

Setting the Agenda

Building the Agreement

Writing the Agreement

Closing Statement

Multiple Sessions

Wrap-Up

❑ PREPARING YOURSELF

If possible, review the case with the person who arranged the mediation and with your co-mediator a day or two ahead of time. For an informal mediation, think through potential problems and strategies you may use.

Be there early enough that you feel relaxed and have time to shift your attention to the mediation. Review the skills and approaches you want to use this time. Remind yourself why you are committed to mediation.

❑ BEFORE THE PARTICIPANTS ARRIVE

Before the participants arrive (and be forewarned that nervous disputants may arrive 10 or 15 minutes early):

➢ Arrange the room: chairs, tables, lighting, room temperature, privacy; extra room for separate meetings or waiting, papers in order, flip chart set up, etc.

➢ Review the case notes, memorize people's names.

➢ Discuss how the mediators will work together.

➢ Check the facilities: know the smoking and parking regulations, and where the bathrooms and telephone are.

➢ Space for Separate Meetings: What second room can you use either to speak privately with someone or have one party to wait while you speak with the other?

❑ DISCUSS WITH YOUR CO-MEDIATOR

Discuss with your co-mediator:

➢ Dividing tasks: Opening Statement, writing out the agreement, facilitating different portions of the session.

➢ Your personal mediation style, what you do well, what you do not do as well, anything you'd like the other mediator to watch for.

➢ How you want to handle Separate Meetings. Also, where and when might the mediators have a separate consultation with each other?

➢ Seating arrangements.

➢ Potential difficulties with the upcoming mediation.

PREPARATION

❑ MEETING THE PARTIES

Greet each person and try to set them at ease, but also refrain from chatting too much. If another party arrives and sees you in friendly conversation, they may wonder if you are impartial.

If one party does not come and you cannot reach them by phone, wait for longer than you normally would (especially if you do not know the person or the person is coming to a new location).

Once you decide to cancel the mediation, the parties that did come may want to consult with you, or you may want to refer them to another agency. If you are mediating for a program, ask for guidelines about handling this conversation. If you are mediating on your own, be careful that your sympathy or suggestions will not fuel the fires (*The mediator said your behavior is illegal!*) or cross the line into giving legal advice. In either case, if you want to eventually mediate the matter, don't discuss substantive issues.

❑ SEATING ARRANGEMENTS

Seating sends strong nonverbal cues to people about what to expect and how to behave in a new environment. Arrangements will differ with the facilities, the number of parties, the degree of animosity, the type of dispute, the cultural background and personalities of the disputants. Whether you are mediating alone, in pairs, or in a team, here are some key factors to consider:

➤ Everyone should be able to see and hear everyone else and participate easily in discussions.

➤ Members of one party should be able to sit together if they choose. Couples typically want to sit side by side.

➤ Everyone should be physically comfortable, undistracted, and feel as safe as possible.

➤ The mediators should be able to control the process.

➤ The seating should suggest mediator impartiality.

➤ Pick a location that feels comfortable and private: not too large, not too dim or cluttered.

The diagrams on the next pages assume two mediators, a party of two (a couple, for instance) and a party of one. We recommend using the Facing, Corner, or Diagonal arrangements described on the next page unless the shape of the table, the size of the group, or the dispute history suggest one of the alternative arrangements.

SEATING ARRANGEMENTS

A. The Round Table

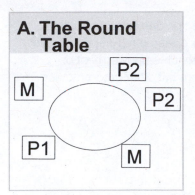

Egalitarian—the round table. A round or square table big enough to accommodate all participants, but not much larger, is ideal if you want to minimize status differences.

B. Distance

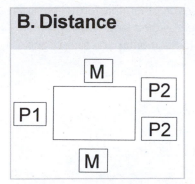

Distance. Using a table, placing a mediator between the parties, or just distancing the chairs can help provide a sense of safety, especially if you suspect some people are feeling intimidated or physically threatened.

C. Living Room

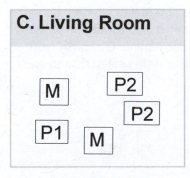

Closeness—the living room arrangement. In other situations you may wish to encourage people to let down their guard by foregoing a table, creating a more homey environment, bringing chairs closer together.

D. Head of the Table

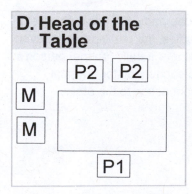

Mediator authority #1—head of the table. By sitting at the head of a rectangular table, mediators can communicate authority and encourage parties to speak to the mediator rather than to each other (which may sometimes be desirable, other times not).

SEATING ARRANGEMENTS

E. The Panel

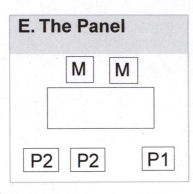

Mediator authority #2—the panel. Sit on one side of the table, facing the parties as in a courtroom or classroom. Friends Conflict Resolution Programs, with its emphasis on empowerment of disputants, has discouraged this pattern but other programs use mediation panels successfully.

F. Facing

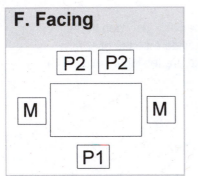

Facing. When parties sit across from each other, this formal position can suggest a "face-off" or "my side versus their side" feeling. Yet it also encourages the parties to speak to each other and to recognize the mediation as a serious, formal session.

G. Corner

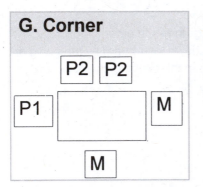

Corner. When parties sit at right angles, it is easier for them to choose how much they look at each other. It also allows mediators to look at both parties without too much head turning. Obviously, you cannot use this seating if the parties feel unsafe seated next to each other.

H. Diagonal

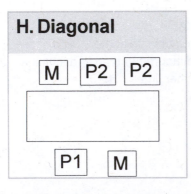

Diagonal. When a mediator sits near one party, or finds it physically easier to give attention to one of the parties, the participants (or even the mediators) may feel that the mediator is literally "on that person's side." The diagonal arrangement gives each mediator physical proximity to one disputant and visual connection to the other.

M = Mediator   P1 = Party #1   P2 = Party #2 (there are two people in this party)

THE OPENING STATEMENT

1. Welcome and words of encouragement

2. Purpose of the mediation; mediator's role

3. Forms and logistics

4. Confidentiality

5. What will happen

6. Separate Meetings

7. Willingness to go ahead

❑ PURPOSE

The Opening Statement sets the tone of the mediation. This is the time to establish your presence and your control of the mediation process. Look around the table as you speak, making connection with each person.

The Opening Statement gives the parties a sense of the mediators and how the process works. It also gives them a moment to get used to sitting in the same room with their adversaries.

❑ GIVING THE OPENING STATEMENT

Keep the Opening Statement short. Nervous or upset participants may not take in much information. Also, do not assume that they remember what they were told about the mediation beforehand.

Divide the Opening Statement between the mediators, or have one person present the information with the co-mediator filling in any gaps. Note that when one person gives the full Opening Statement, it implies that she or he is the lead mediator.

OPENING STATEMENT

Although the Opening Statement should touch on each of the following topics, you can adapt the amount of detail and the sequence of the points to your own style and to the particular context of a mediation. If you are new to mediation, we recommend rehearsing several times until you can be succinct and confident.

1. Welcome and words of encouragement

Welcome people individually. If some people haven't met before, repeat the names of the mediators and of the parties, and ask how people wish to be addressed. Write their names on your notepad.

Keep in mind that disputants may be tense, wary, skeptical, or ready to make a scene. Mediation is an unknown for them. They are sitting across the table from people they do not like. They may be asked to speak about their own faults and mistakes.

Compliment them on their courage to try something difficult and unfamiliar. Reassure them that although mediation is not easy, in your experience it can often make difficult situations much better.

2. Purpose of the mediation, the mediator's role

Explain that you are present to help people talk to each other constructively and find their own solutions.

Review what organization you represent or why you were asked to mediate. If someone else arranged the mediation, explain that you are not the person they spoke with earlier.

Note that mediators are not judges; you cannot determine the facts about what has happened, you will not be judging who is at fault, you will not be telling them how to fix the situation.

Emphasize that everyone will be looking at how to improve the situation from now on.

3. Forms and logistics

Give them time to review and sign any required participation forms.

Note the location of the water fountain, bathrooms, and explain smoking regulations. Assure them that they may ask for a break when they need it.

Remind them how long you expect the session to take. If they say they can't stay that long, do not press the point. Just say, *Let's see how far we get by 9:30, and then we'll check in to see how much longer you can stay.* Mention the possibility of multiple sessions.

4. Confidentiality

Explain that the *mediators* will keep confidential what happens in the mediation. Summarize briefly what this means in practice. (See pages 76, 154-5.) If anyone raises concerns about the *participants* keeping the session confidential, the parties can include that in their agreement.

5. What will happen

Outline the mediation procedure briefly, emphasizing that at the beginning each participant will have a turn to speak without interruption. If they come to agreement, the mediators will write it down, everyone will sign it, and everyone will get a copy to take home.

Stress that the agreement will be theirs; you will not press them to sign *anything* they don't fully agree to.

6. Separate Meetings

Explain that mediators may ask at some point to speak individually with the parties or to consult with each other. Also, anyone may ask for a Separate Meeting if they want to confer with other members of their party or with the mediators. Reassure them that mediators will keep confidential anything said in a Separate Meeting.

This information is important to state up front, so that no one feels startled or chastised when the mediator decides to hold Separate Meetings. Present Separate Meetings as a normal part of the mediation process.

7. Willingness to go ahead

Check whether they have any questions or concerns.

Then ask if they are willing to proceed with the session with you as mediators, and get assent from each party before beginning Uninterrupted Time.

UNINTERRUPTED TIME

> ## UNINTERRUPTED TIME
>
> 1. Set a courteous, unhurried tone
>
> 2. Explain listening and speaking
>   - Each person will have a turn to speak
>   - Listen to what each person has to say
>
> 3. Select someone to start
>
> 4. Protect each person's speaking time
>
> 5. Formally end each turn: check that the person is finished, thank them, move on

❑ PURPOSE

Uninterrupted Time gives everyone at the table—the mediators and the parties—a chance to hear each person's story. The mediators get an overview of the situation and a sense of the individual personalities involved. Equally importantly, each person has an opportunity to explain their point of view and express their feelings without interruption or challenge.

1. Set a courteous, unhurried tone

The Uninterrupted Time phase gives mediators another opportunity to set a serious, respectful mood where people can begin listening to each other and speaking honestly.

For this reason, try to start Uninterrupted Time without lots of rules and expectations—just ask them to listen without interrupting as if you assume that, of course, they will. You can invoke strong groundrules later if interrupting or rudeness proves to be a problem. If you are mediating a large group, however, or you see that the parties are already provoking or interrupting each other, you may want to lay out more detailed groundrules up front.

2. Explain listening and speaking

Instead of using the awkward term "Uninterrupted Time" with the parties, simply say that you will start by giving each person a turn to speak.

> **Ask listeners:**

We ask you to respect each person's turn to speak even though it may be hard for you to listen without responding right away.

You can jot a note to yourself about anything you want to bring up later.

Listen for anything new, for something you didn't know before.

> **Ask speakers an open-ended question:**

Can you tell us about the situation from your point of view?

What's been happening and how does it affect you?

3. Select someone to start

The person who is most agitated or seems to have the main complaint can start, or you can ask who wants to go first and see who volunteers. If you pick, just say *Alex, why don't you start?* without further explanations of why you chose Alex.

4. Protect each person's speaking time

When, as often happens, those listening cannot contain themselves from commenting, demonstrate that you are consistent and fair, and that you will protect each person's turn.

If someone is very upset by what another party is saying or is anxious during their own turn, reassure them that they will have plenty of chance to talk during the mediation.

For those incapable of staying quiet, state the groundrules explicitly, then cope as best you can. Try not to let the interrupter draw away your attention from the speaker.

Tom, you had (will have) your turn. Please respect Sally's.

Jill, I know it is hard to listen to this. Please write down what you want to say so that you remember to bring it up during your turn.

If interruptions continue despite your quiet reminders, get tough and insist they stop. Get the person's explicit verbal agreement to refrain from interrupting. (See the Controlling the Process section.)

UNINTERRUPTED TIME

Hold off on asking questions

Respect the "No interrupting" rule yourself. You are the model for the participants. There will be plenty of time to clear up confusions during the Exchange phase.

Sometimes you will need to say something to help draw out people who are reluctant or don't know what to say. Sometimes it helps to remind them that you need information since you haven't spoken with them before.

Ask people to speak to the mediators

If the parties are interrupting each other or starting active discussion, ask the speaker to address the mediators for now. It is difficult for anyone to listen silently when directly questioned or attacked.

Frank: ...and you threatened to smash my car windows. Didn't you? Then you have the nerve to deny it to the police! I could ...

Eric, interrupting: How dare you accuse me? It was you who...

*Mediator: Eric, it's still Frank's turn. Frank, can you explain the situation to **me**? It is hard for Eric not to answer you back.*

5. Formally end each speaker's turn

At the end of each person's turn, inquire whether the speaker has anything else to say right now, and then thank them. Do not comment, ask questions, or summarize yet. If the other party had difficulty waiting for their turn, thank them for their patience.

Turns: how long, how many?

A time limit for turns is not necessary unless you have more than six or seven people. If someone is excessively detailed or long-winded, step in to end their turn when they begin repeating themselves.

You can call for a second round if the first speakers said much less than the people who followed or if you think that a more open discussion will be difficult to control.

THE EXCHANGE

1. Keep control of the session

2. Include each person

3. Ask necessary questions

4. Listen for interests and issues

5. Refrain from finding solutions yet

6. Watch for moments of understanding or reconciliation

7. Summarize their interests and concerns

❑ PURPOSE

The Exchange is an open discussion period where the parties respond to each other's Uninterrupted Time statements and explore information, perceptions, and feelings. During this time, both the mediators and the parties fill in information gaps and come to understand what the main issues, obstacles, and possibilities are.

The Exchange is a structured, protected opportunity for people to:

➢ Speak openly and to express strong feelings and beliefs.

➢ Ask questions and respond to each other's accusations and perceptions.

The Exchange is primarily about helping the parties move towards reconciliation—that point when (at least tacitly) they begin to acknowledge each other's perspectives and needs. With that foundation, the parties can then attend to resolving particular issues during Building the Agreement.

THE EXCHANGE

❑ Directing the Exchange

The mediator's challenge in the Exchange is directing the discussion of very different perspectives and intense feelings. It can be difficult to resist their desire and yours to plunge right away into the calmer, more rational waters of problem-solving.

The mediators wear many hats during the Exchange. They try to keep people's emotional reactions within bounds and direct sometimes chaotic conversational traffic. At the same time they are building rapport and helping the disputants listen to each other, the mediators are also asking for information and listening closely to the details of the dispute. Throughout, they watch for any small seedlings of potential reconciliation, gently trying to make room for them to grow.

Starting the Exchange

If discussion does not begin spontaneously after Uninterrupted Time, the mediators can simply indicate that the discussion is now open to everyone. Sometimes you will want to focus the conversation, starting off by addressing one person or asking for basic information:

➤ *Thank you all for your patience. I have a lot of questions to ask, and I'm sure you do too.*

➤ *Geraldine, can you say more about _____?*

➤ *Can someone sketch the layout of your properties for me?*

> ### Clearing it out
>
> *The Exchange is like cleaning out your closets… It looks like a huge mess and you wonder how you'll ever organize it. But you have to start by dumping all the stuff out and seeing what is there.*
>
> *—Chel Avery*

© 1997 Friends Conflict Resolution Programs

Keep control of the session

The Exchange can call on all your facilitation skills. At times the session may seem out of control. Often mediators can ride out this stormy period unless you feel a party is being abusive or preventing someone from participating fully. Usually people will run out of steam. If not, taking a break or having Separate Meetings can help lower the intensity level.

Mediators learn to wait out the roller coaster up and downs of the Exchange. However the parties, who are already nervous, may worry that you are not keeping the discussion in hand. Projecting your own ease and confidence can help. At times you may need to acknowledge aloud that they are uncomfortable, and reassure them that volatile discussions are normal during this part of the mediation session.

For dealing with particularly hot situations, review the section on Controlling the Process.

Include each person

Be careful to include each person and emphasize that everyone's input is important. Even if a person dominating the conversation has many useful things to say, you can still break in pleasantly:

> *Peter, can you hold it there for a minute? I want to hear reactions to what you've said and then we'll get back to you.*

Don't forget, you can always call Separate Meetings, either to confront a person who is disrupting or to support someone who is having difficulty participating.

Accept but don't press for emotions

Many feelings will come up: resentment, hatred, frustration, jealousy, fear, outrage, grief. In judging whether to contain an emotional outburst, ask yourself, "Will this help the mediation?" (See Should I Intervene? on page 92.) Airing feelings can help people resolve or even transform their conflicts and this is why mediators try to make room for the disputants to express themselves. When the mediators take tears or angry outbursts in stride, they show that strong feelings are understandable, expected, and will not derail the session.

However, it is up to each individual to decide how much emotion they want to reveal. Do not press them to talk about their feelings. They are the ones who have to live with the consequences of what they say.

THE EXCHANGE

Ask necessary questions

➤ Gather *only* the information you need to understand people's interests and what kinds of agreements are likely to work.

➤ Good questions help everyone at the table understand the situation better.

➤ Make sure that your questions do not continuously direct the discussion; the parties know best what topics are most important. (See Asking the Right Questions, 106-7.)

➤ If the parties are talking past each other because they have very different concerns, write up all the questions they would like answered during this session. Summarize what seems most important to know. Only then have them answer the questions.

Listen for interests and issues

Listen carefully for people's interests—what really matters to them. Also keep notes on the issues raised, along with obstacles and potential solutions. (See Taking Notes, 105; and Interests, 110-12.)

Help the parties. By judicious restating, clarifying, and summarizing, you can help them get a clearer idea of each other's interests and issues, too.

Refrain from finding solutions yet

Because the Exchange can seem disorganized and the gap between the parties too wide for bridge-building, this is often the most anxious time in the mediation, both for the parties and for the mediators.

Consequently, the fragrant whiff of a possible solution can easily distract the mediators, who may sometimes shortchange the Exchange phase in their eagerness to resolve the conflict. The parties, who are probably also uncomfortable, may willingly follow the mediator's lead into discussing solutions.

The trouble is, if you explore solutions now you may reach agreements that don't address the significant problems or don't meet each party's interests. You may also find yourself coping with acrimonious exchanges which re-emerge late in the mediation.

Wait until you have a good grasp of the larger picture: the issues, the interests. Also, the parties need significant time to air their grievances before they are emotionally ready to start Building the Agreement. Note down the possible solution and raise it again later.

❏ THE TURNING POINT

Watch for moments of understanding or reconciliation

Occasionally after an intense Exchange there is a moment we call the "Turning Point." Someone makes an apology, someone offers a concession or a kind word. The room falls silent. Then, like water rushing through a breach in the dam, comes an outpouring of personal sharing, of ideas and offers.

This dramatic shift from accusations and defensiveness to empathy and resolution is what mediation at its best is all about. It is not something you as mediator can make happen, but you can watch for it, make room for it, then move gently on to discussing the mundane details of the agreement.

Summarize their interests and concerns

When to bring the Exchange to a close is a judgment call. One signal is when the parties begin to shift their conversation from what happened yesterday to what should happen tomorrow.

End with a summary acknowledging the interests and concerns you have heard and, if the subject is not too delicate, recognize the parties' feelings or Turning Point as well.

> I think you now have a better idea what this disagreement has meant to the other party. This past month seems to have been difficult for everyone. Len, your main concern seems to be having control over your own decisions and getting respect for your skill. And Kyle, you are worried about liability and want Len to understand that you are trying to be responsible and responsive. Is that right? (Look to each person for confirmation or correction.)

This summary acknowledgment can lead directly into the Setting the Agenda phase, which begins with a review of what the parties have accomplished during the Exchange discussion.

SEPARATE MEETINGS

❑ WHEN TO USE SEPARATE MEETINGS

Separate Meetings are private conversations with each party. Mediators may ask for Separate Meetings at *any* time during the mediation, for example when the mediators need to:

1. Support the people

➢ Separate, cool off, or calm down people who are distraught or in a rage.

➢ Give a shy or fearful person a chance to talk.

➢ Help people think through what they want or need.

2. Control the process

➢ Change the mood or direction of the session.

➢ Interrupt unhelpful behaviors such as attacking, withdrawing, namecalling, stonewalling.

➢ Confront people privately.

3. Solve the problem

➢ Receive private information.

➢ Explore interests and potential solutions.

➢ Help get the discussion unstuck.

4. Consult with your co-mediator

➢ Strategize.

➢ Confer on an issue checklist before Setting the Agenda.

➢ Talk through disagreements between you.

➢ Raise concerns about impartiality.

SEPARATE MEETINGS

❏ PREPARING FOR SEPARATE MEETINGS

Before the mediation starts

➢ Decide where Separate Meetings will take place and where the other parties will wait.

➢ Will mediators stay together and speak with parties in turn, or split up with each talking to one party? We recommend that mediators talk jointly with each party. Splitting up may sometimes be a better strategy: for instance if you have many parties, if you think one party cannot be left to wait alone, if people seem weary of the process, or if one mediator has established rapport with a difficult disputant.

Calling a Separate Meeting

➢ **Always meet with each party** so that you stay impartial. At times you may want to ask permission to meet with one person alone (say a teenager who has come with her parents). Just make sure you meet with the rest of the party later.

➢ Call for separate meetings in a matter-of-fact tone and (this can be hard) without explanations or justifications.

➢ Be clear in your own mind about the purpose of this conversation and what you want to accomplish with each party.

➢ Give the waiting parties something to do. Tell them how long you will be and remember to check in if you're running longer.

➢ Take your notes with you if you leave the table.

A comment about hesitations

In practice, mediators may hesitate to call a Separate Meeting.

They have momentum, they're getting somewhere. It is important to be sensitive to "flow." Recognize also, however, people's need for a mental and emotional break during an intense session.

One of the disputants may simply leave if there is a break. If things are that tense, you *need* to have a private discussion. Have one mediator talk with each party so that no one has to wait.

Face-to-face negotiation is the best way to resolve conflicts. Try using Separate Meetings to help individuals prepare to negotiate more respectfully, creatively, and honestly.

SEPARATE MEETINGS

> ## SEPARATE MEETINGS
>
> 1. Assure them of confidentiality
>
> 2. We wanted to talk with you about _____
>
> 3. Stay focused
>
> 4. Be understanding but impartial
>
> 5. Check what you are permitted to say to others
>
> 6. When we go back to the table _____

SEPARATE MEETINGS

1. Assure them of confidentiality

State that you will not repeat anything they say during the Separate Meeting without their permission.

2. We wanted to talk to you about _____

Tell them what you want to discuss in this Separate Meeting:

We wanted to check whether there's anything else you'd like us to know.

I'm not sure you want to be here.

I wanted to discuss the solution you proposed.

3. Stay focused

Keep in mind why you are meeting and don't get sidetracked unless something important comes up. The other parties should not have to wait too long.

4. Be understanding but impartial

Tell them you know the situation is hard, that it can be difficult to know what to do. Be careful, though, that you do not appear to support their position, accept their assessment of the situation, or become their advocate.

5. Check what you are permitted to say to others

Ask what parts of the conversation they will permit you to repeat at the table or privately to another party. If you must carry a message to another party, make it clear that you are doing so with express permission.

Jacob asked me to see whether you'd be willing to consider talking to him without your wife present.

6. When we go back to the table

If at all possible, persuade them to speak directly rather than have you carry messages or speak for them when you return to the table.

Confirm out loud what will happen next. For example, reaffirm that they agree to make an offer or to stick to the subject on the table, or that you agree to keep the other party from interrupting.

SETTING THE AGENDA

SETTING THE AGENDA

1. Summarize what has been accomplished so far

2. List the issues they need to negotiate

3. Agree on an agenda

4. If useful, agree on guidelines for subsequent discussion and decision-making

❑ PURPOSE

In Setting the Agenda, mediators reframe complaints and concerns as a set of issues for problem-solving. This stage may only take five minutes, but it is crucial for defining the issues and organizing how they will be discussed.

Together with the participants, the mediators *define* the problem and start to create common ground for negotiation. The mediator has considerable discretion in this part of the mediation.

1. Summarize what has been accomplished so far

At the end of the Exchange, you acknowledged the perspectives and feelings of the parties. You can follow this with the first step in Setting the Agenda: a brief review of what they have accomplished so far in moving towards reconciliation and/or resolutions.

You've spent a productive hour hearing each other's concerns and clearing up several miscommunications. You both agree that you'd like to finish this project and that you need to figure out who oversees which aspects of the production before you go any further. Are you ready to look at specifics now?

2. List the issues

First, organize your notes and select key issues

At the close of the Exchange phase, mediators distill the parties' many comments and concerns into a few important and negotiable topics.

Concentrate on issues with these characteristics:

➢ Need a joint decision.

➢ Mentioned frequently.

➢ Have emotional charge.

➢ Potentially negotiable.

➢ Key to a lasting resolution.

End the list with the one issue that belongs on most mediation agendas: *How do the parties want to handle any future problems or tensions?*

THE ISSUE CHECKLIST

➢ **States the topics that need to be discussed.**

➢ **Uses positive, impartial language.**

➢ **Reflects each person's concerns.**

➢ **Presents problems as shared concerns whenever possible.**

➢ **Is succinct and easy to recall.**

SETTING THE AGENDA

Word each issue carefully

Describe each issue using words that are impartial, yet meaningful for all parties. For example, use: *How problems with customers are handled* works better than the biased: *Jane's problem with Polly's sales manner*, or the vague, all-purpose *communication problems*.

Pages 115-119 offer more details about defining and grouping issues, reframing issues in neutral language, and finding the negotiable elements of non-mediatable issues.

Read your checklist aloud

One mediator may propose an issue checklist, with the other mediator and participants amending it. Or the mediators can call a five-minute stretch to consult with each other, then present it jointly.

If you don't write the checklist on the board, tick off each topic with your fingers as you speak to reinforce each separate item on the list. Use a brief phrase for each topic, then explain what concerns come under each issue.

> *The second issue is Co-op member hours. That includes deciding how to credit volunteer time, and also concerns about people doing their fair share of less popular tasks.*

3. Agree on an agenda

Check for accuracy and completeness

If possible, write the agenda topics on a board where all can see.

Ask: *Is this list accurate? Does it cover all the important issues?* If the issues list is long, get a sense of which items they think need priority.

From the list, finalize an agenda. What will you cover in this session and in what order? How long will it probably take? Let them know that the *order* may change as you go along.

4. Agree on guidelines

In more complex or intense mediations, the mediators may also want to reach agreement with the parties on guidelines for:

➢ How issues will be discussed. (*Talking about payments is off limits today. Everyone will receive copies of all documents. Jim will have an opportunity to check the proposed schedule with his wife before the agreement becomes final.*)

➢ Criteria for acceptable decisions. (*Any agreement will stay within $550. Any solution must not increase current pollution levels.*)

☐ ISSUE CHECKLIST EXAMPLES

During Uninterrupted Time and the Exchange you hear these concerns:	You might list the issues like this:
How dare you expect us to just rubberstamp your decision! You talk to your buddies but ignore the rest of us. I won't be bulldozed into letting this budget pass until we've talked about each and every line. Some people just can't deal with any change. No matter what we propose you always moan and roll your eyes but make no constructive suggestions. Furthermore you haven't done a lick of work for this committee for years except to throw sand in the gears.	■ **These sound like the main topics we need to talk about tonight:** ✓ **Committee decisions—how they are made** ✓ **Committee member responsibilities** ✓ **How you deal with differences.** **Any additions or changes?**
Don't you dare tell my kids you are going to smack them! You are the adult, control yourself! If you have a problem, you come to ME. Got it? Your kids are brats! They are completely undisciplined. They push other kids, scratch and hit, and don't listen to adults who tell them to stop.	■ **I think these are the main issues:** ✓ **Who disciplines kids and how** ✓ **How to communicate with each other when problems with kids come up** ✓ **What behavior on the playground is not okay.** **Does this sound right to you?**
When you talk to me, I expect some respect. You are the secretary, not the manager around here. If I tell you to get this project in the mail, then that's what you're supposed to do. This half-assed job is unacceptable! You aren't my supervisor, John is. *He* is the one who assigns my work, not you. I don't care if you have been here ten years and have a fancy title. Put your request in the in-box just like everyone else has to. Don't dump your work on me!	■ **Here are the possible agenda topics for our discussion:** 1. **Who assigns the secretary's work** 2. **How to communicate about work tasks, schedules, quality of work** 3. **How the two of you treat each other.** **Can we deal with all 3 topics in the next hour?**

BUILDING THE AGREEMENT

> ## BUILDING THE AGREEMENT
>
> 1. Work through each issue in turn:
>   - ➤ Elicit ideas
>   - ➤ Evaluate and refine alternatives
>   - ➤ Test for agreement and explore consequences
>   - ➤ Write down tentative agreements
>
> 2. Keep discussion on track

❑ PURPOSE

While solving problems is not the only goal of mediation, it is probably the main reason the parties have come to mediation. The Building the Agreement phase is the time for parties to:

➤ Identify and evaluate a range of ideas.

➤ Negotiate with everyone's interests in mind.

➤ Develop and test specific proposals.

➤ Gain confidence in their ability to resolve the situation and to build commitment to the emerging agreement.

Their problems need *their* solutions

How much leadership does the mediator take in finding workable solutions? Because we encourage people to control their own lives, and because we want parties to uphold their agreements, our mediators provide a process and let disputants provide solutions. (For more on this philosophy, see pages 8-9 and 122.)

There is no single right way to organize problem-solving. We outline one straightforward approach below, with more details and examples in the section on Solving the Problem.

BUILDING THE AGREEMENT

❑ WORKING THROUGH AN ISSUE

Select an issue from the agenda

Start with an issue that matters to *both* parties and either is easy to resolve or is the issue that seems key to all the rest. During the discussion, you may need to either focus on or expand the subject. If they bog down on one issue, leave it aside and move on to another.

Elicit options

For each issue in turn:

➤ Get a number of suggestions before discussing their merits.

➤ Ask what they are already doing that works.

➤ Ask what each person can offer that the other party might accept.

Evaluate and refine alternatives

Weed out solutions that seem unworkable. For the most promising solutions, press the parties to answer all these questions:

➤ What are the advantages? Disadvantages?

➤ Possible consequences?

➤ Does it meet everyone's interests?

➤ Can people realistically carry it out?

Test for agreement and explore consequences

Check (privately if need be) that each person agrees to the proposed solution. Leave people room to back down if they seem uneasy with it. Explore the possible consequences, especially if you question whether the solution will work. Be aware that some may be agreeing quickly just to be done with the mediation.

Write down tentative agreements

In your own notes, record their tentative agreement or summarize the area of disagreement. Leave the final polishing to the Writing the Agreement phase when you are considering the agreement as a whole; the parties may want to change elements of this preliminary agreement as they work out other issues.

BUILDING THE AGREEMENT

❑ GUIDING THE DISCUSSION

Keep the discussion on track

During Building the Agreement, the mediators' main task is to structure and referee the problem-solving part of the mediation.

➢ **Expect some tacking back and forth** between related issues and moments where emotions flare and the parties are back in Exchange-mode for a while. As mediator you need to judge when these directions are productive and when to return to a focus on a single issue.

➢ **Refer back to the agenda** when you need to keep the discussion on track.

We're working on the salary issue right now. The Co-op member hours issue is next. Is there something I should note down so we remember to discuss it then?

➢ **Keep an eye on the clock** and how fast you are moving through the agenda. People's energies ebb quickly and you want to use their time together to focus on the most significant issues.

On the other hand, if they keep returning to a "small" issue when you want to move on, double-check with them about what their priorities are.

➢ **Use a flipchart or blackboard.** If you have several disputants, a complex agenda, or if someone has trouble following what has been said, post a list of issues under discussion and/or tentative areas of agreement for everyone to see.

WRITING THE AGREEMENT

> ## WRITING THE AGREEMENT
>
> 1. Review each point of agreement:
>   - Workable?
>   - Wording okay?
>   - Acceptable?
>
> 2. Write out the final copy, read it out loud
>
> 3. Have everyone present sign and give each party a copy

❑ PURPOSE

The written agreement:

- Gives tangible evidence that parties accomplished something together.
- Reminds people what they agreed to.
- Helps prevent arguments and misunderstandings afterward.
- Gives a clear ending point to the mediation process.

"Do we have to write it down?"

Well, yes, there are good reasons to insist that disputing parties write down their agreements. Be prepared for resistance, though, especially when people have close relationships or come from cultures which customarily resolve disagreements with verbal promises. For these people, writing down an agreement can feel uncomfortably formal. It suggests a continuing lack of trust, the fragility of their promises. If they are fearful of locking themselves into promises they might not want to keep, you can propose an interim agreement or a time period for them to check with lawyers or others before finalizing the agreement.

The reality is that serious disputes do not vanish completely after a two hour session. A written agreement helps their promises take root.

WRITING THE AGREEMENT

❏ THE FINAL REVIEW

At this point the mediators and the parties feel the urge to hurry and be done. However, when people go back to their daily routines the agreement may be the only thing that helps them sustain the progress they made during the mediation. Make *sure* that the parties understand it and are committed to it.

1. Review each point of agreement: Is it Workable? Wording okay? Acceptable?

Before you write a point of agreement on the final copy, read your draft out loud. Check that people think it is realistic, that they like the wording, and that they can agree to it.

Be forewarned that even at this last moment, a sudden case of "cold feet" is common as it hits people what they are agreeing to and what they are giving up. Try not to panic!

➢ Remind them of the consequences of omitting that point of the agreement.

➢ Acknowledge that they are each taking risks and each offering something.

➢ Reaffirm that you do not want them to sign anything unless they *fully* agree to it.

➢ Listen carefully to their unease to determine if the agreement does not meet that person's interests or feels alien to their customary style.

➢ If it is a minor point, ask them to put this item aside for a moment while you finalize the others.

➢ If necessary, go back to the Building Agreement phase.

2. Write out the final copy, read it aloud

If you can, draw up a final copy during the session. Read the completed clean copy out loud, watching to make sure that each person follows and agrees. Be sensitive to the fact that some people may have difficulty reading or writing quickly.

3. Have everyone present sign, give each party a copy

The parties sign to show their agreement. Mediators and any support people sign as participants and witnesses.

WRITING THE AGREEMENT

❏ **SAMPLE AGREEMENT**

MEDIATION AGREEMENT

Date: 6/5/99   Time: Wed. evening
                      Place: Colwyn Center

Mediators: Malcom James, Janine McClain

Names: Harry Harridan   Cliff Clifford

Address: #32 D Streeet   #32 D Street
         Anywhere, IN   Anywhere, IN

---

1. Harry and Cliff agree that they want the apartment to feel like home for <u>both</u> of them.

2. Both agree to have a check-in time every Thursday, 5:30PM.

3. Cliff agrees to buy his own laundry hamper tomorrow.

4. Both agree to quiet hours:

   Sun--Thurs: After 11PM

   Sat--Sun: Before 11:30 AM

5. Harry agrees to clean his dishes before 8PM.

6. Cliff agrees to leave a note on the table if Marjorie plan to stay over the <u>next</u> night. On school nights, they will visit in Cliff's room unless Harry invites them to join him.

7. Both agree to ask permission before using the other person's food or CDs or desk supplies.

Signed: _Cliff Clifford_   _Harry Harridan_

Mediators: _Janine McClain_   _Malcolm James_

WRITING THE AGREEMENT

❏ WRITING A STURDY AGREEMENT

The written agreement will be the only record of what happened during the mediation. The way you construct that document can help make sure that all bases have been covered and that everyone takes home a clear and positive statement of their decisions. (More sample agreements are on pages 125-6.)

A GOOD WRITTEN AGREEMENT

1. **Details specifics: who, what, when.**

2. **Is evenhanded and not conditional.**

3. **Uses clear, familiar wording.**

4. **Emphasizes positive action.**

5. **Deals with any pending proceedings.**

6. **Provides for the future.**

---

1. Details specifics: who, what, when

Cover all the details. Thus, *Mrs. Wrangle and the McBickers agree to build a fence* is less satisfactory than:

> *Mrs. Wrangle and the McBickers agree to build a 5-foot high board fence 24 inches in from their joint property line on Mrs. Wrangle's side. Mrs. Wrangle agrees to buy the lumber and the McBickers agree to construct the fence. Mrs. Wrangle will own the fence.*

➢ Set times and deadlines:

> *Mrs. Wrangle will buy the lumber no later than May 8, and the McBickers will finish the fence before May 30. Both parties agree to have their own side of the fence painted by June 28th.*

> The less possibility for misunderstanding afterward, the better. Therefore, the agreement should clearly state:

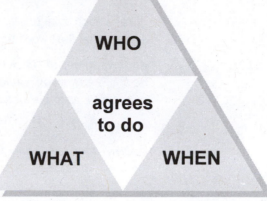

2. Is evenhanded and not conditional

Ideally, all parties give something, all parties gain. Try not to have six paragraphs that start: *Judy agrees to _____*, and only one *Richard agrees to ___*. Emphasize their mutual actions when you can: *Everyone agrees to _____*.

Try not to make one person's promises contingent on another party's actions (or else the whole agreement may come unravelled).

Marcie agrees to clean the storeroom Friday mornings.
Randy agrees to do the inventory Friday afternoons.

Is better than: *Randy agrees to do inventory if Marcie cleans the storeroom on time.*

3. Uses clear, familiar wording

Use the parties' words whenever possible. Make short, straight-forward sentences. Avoid bureaucratic or legalistic language. If the dispute involves legal issues, the parties can arrange for a lawyer to draft a legal document based on the mediation agreement.

Watch for ambiguous words (For example, respect, friendly, soon, will take care of, reasonable, cooperative, neighborly, frequent, communicate, quiet). Any statement that can be interpreted more than one way may spark fresh misunderstandings later.

4. Emphasizes positive action

➤ Emphasize that they have *agreed* by starting each item of agreement with the phrase

(The Dawsons) **agree to** _____.

➤ Phrase each point to say what parties agree they *will* do, rather than stating what they won't do or will stop doing. Thus,

Andrew agrees to check with Carla at least two days before he takes any action. Carla agrees to keep phone conversations to business topics only.

is better than:

Andrew must check with Carla before taking any action. Andrew will not hang up when he doesn't like what Carla is saying.

5. Deals with any pending proceedings

If the parties are also involved in formal proceedings such as a court suit, a grievance procedure, a custody hearing, an inquiry, or a discipline process, the agreement should state what will happen to those proceedings. If the parties agree to drop a court case, make sure they know the procedure for doing so.

Dealing with this is *very* important. If they do not resolve this issue, it will almost certainly undermine any goodwill built up during the mediation and nullify the agreement.

6. Provides for the future

How will the parties communicate if more problems arise? In the rush of good feeling—or just plain relief—that can come at the end of a mediation, people often insist that there will be no more problems. Press them anyway. Will they make visits in person? Send notes? Telephone? Use a go-between?

This provision is a vital safety valve. It gives people an excuse and a method for bringing up a concern with the other party. It also helps the mediators when parties complain later that the other side is not honoring the agreement. If you ask them whether they have contacted the other party and the answer is no, you can encourage them to follow their agreement by first trying to address the situation directly.

❏ AGREEMENT VARIATIONS

Statements of principle or shared point of view

Sometimes the parties agree on a point of view, rather than on an action. Include it if you think it will remind them of why they want to uphold the agreement.

Everyone agreed that they want to get this product to market.

All present agree that Rita has done a wonderful job taking care of the membership drive.

Walt and Olga agree that it is very important for their children to have two active parents, and they will make parenting decisions based on this principle.

Fred and Tina agree that the current contract is acceptable as it stands, with the following two exceptions: …

Word these agreements about principles in a way that doesn't set people up to accuse each other of breaking them. For instance, you wouldn't want to write:

Everyone agrees to be friendly with each other.

After the mediation, people may disagree about whether the other party is indeed being "friendly." Instead, you can write:

Everyone agrees that they want a friendly office environment.
(Follow with specific behavior agreements towards that goal.)

Mediation Session Summary

When the parties have only reached a partial agreement or none at all, it can be useful to write up a summary. It is particularly helpful at the end of each session of a multi-session mediation. You may also want to use this in mediations where participants are more comfortable with a meeting minutes format. Note: Only use a summary statement if you think it will not fuel future battles, legal or otherwise.

Walking out with a piece of paper seems to reassure the parties that their effort was not unnoticed or wasted. Write the summary to convey a sense of optimism and accomplishment.

WRITING THE AGREEMENT

A Mediation Session Summary might include these elements:

Mediation Session Summary

Date:
Location:
Names of all persons present:
Mediators:

➢ **The parties reached the following points of agreement:**

➢ **Areas of disagreement yet to be resolved are:**

➢ **We also discussed:**

You can also include non-mediatable topics here, such as:

Carol and Tom discussed what each person meant by "being professional" and the issue of respecting each other.

The teachers spent most of the time talking about how to get more people to next week's meeting.

➢ **Next steps:**

➢ **Date, time, and place of next meeting, if any:**

Signed _____ (parties)

_____

_____ (mediators)

CLOSING STATEMENT

THE CLOSING STATEMENT

1. Acknowledge what they have accomplished

2. Make pay or donation arrangements

3. Review next steps, follow-up

4. Wish them well

❑ PURPOSE

Emotions can be high, even euphoric, at the end of a session. At other times, participants may feel washed out or hopeless—even when from the mediator's perspective the parties have reached a good agreement. The Closing Statement is a time to acknowledge these feelings and bring the session to a positive close.

1. Acknowledge what they have accomplished

Compliment them on their hard work, their willingness to meet and speak frankly, and whatever else deserves recognition.

Review what they have achieved. This can include deciding to come today, learning more about what is important for each person, listening to each other, clearing up some misunderstandings, speaking from the heart, reaching agreement. Don't overdo it; be brief and honest.

If they did not reach agreement, review any progress and points of agreement they did reach.

2. Make pay or donation arrangements

3. Next steps

Remind them of follow-up or second session arrangements. State again their agreement about how they will communicate with each other should more problems come up.

MULTIPLE SESSIONS

❏ SHOULD THEY MEET AGAIN?

Ideally, the person arranging the mediation has determined in advance that this dispute will need several sessions, and the participants will be expecting a more extended process. You may, however, need to make a judgment call during the mediation.

In either case, look for these signs that another session might be most useful:

Timing and logistics

✓ The session has gone on for more than 2 and a half hours.

✓ People seem tired out, distracted.

✓ There are many parties, which means more issues, more constituents who aren't at the table, and more people taking part in the mediation sessions. Logistically, you need more negotiation time.

Some issues are not yet resolved

✓ Many issues, complex or technical issues.

✓ The agreement seems rushed or premature.

✓ There are too many unresolved issues.

✓ The parties want to continue working on reaching agreement.

The people present cannot make a decision

✓ One party is not prepared to negotiate.

✓ A key person or group is not present at the session.

Consultations and information gathering needed

✓ Parties need time to gather more information.

✓ Parties want to consult others (lawyers, constituents, people who will be affected, etc.) before finalizing the agreement.

They want to test possible solutions

✓ Parties want to try out their agreement for a test period, then meet again for evaluation and revisions.

❑ TRANSITIONS BETWEEN SESSIONS

At the end of the first session

Tie up as many loose ends as you can while the parties are still at the table. This reduces the chances of further friction in the interim. Besides, the parties sometimes fail to show up for a scheduled second session.

➢ Make sure that *they* want a second session, not just that the mediators think it is a good idea.

➢ Agree on how people will act in the interim period: What is confidential? How will they treat each other? Do they want to freeze any new actions until the next session? (For instance, you don't want someone to bulldoze a building under contention, escalate a court battle, fire someone, etc. But you might encourage other sorts of initiatives.)

➢ Summarize the progress they have made.

➢ Review tasks that each person agrees to do in the interim.

➢ Double-check the time and place of the next session.

➢ Shortly afterward, prepare a handout summarizing the previous session and listing the unresolved issues on the agenda for the next session. Depending on the nature of the dispute, you may want to send this to participants beforehand.

At the beginning of the next session

➢ Brief in advance any new person who is joining the mediation.

➢ If someone does not come, telephone. Then decide with the other parties whether this session can accomplish anything without that person's presence.

➢ Using a handout or a flipchart, review what they have already resolved, any progress towards agreement, today's proposed agenda.

➢ Ask if there are any suggested changes to the agenda, but do not get into substantive discussion until everyone agrees on the topics for the session.

➢ Start with a round of Uninterrupted Time for each person to report on any progress, new information, or rethinking.

WRAP-UP

> ## WRAP-UP
>
> 1. Complete all paperwork
>
> 2. Evaluate with your co-mediator
>
> 3. Arrange for any follow-up tasks
>
> 4. Keep essential information only; destroy the rest of your notes
>
> 5. Appreciate the hard work you and your co-mediator have done

❑ EVALUATION

Always leave extra time in your schedule to have a thorough discussion with your co-mediator following the mediation. (See pages 156-9 for sample evaluation forms.)

Use this time to clarify and make explicit for yourself what you learned from this particular mediation. It is also a rare opportunity to get useful feedback from a knowledgeable colleague who has just watched you in action. Press yourself to be as receptive and as candid as you can. Future disputants deserve good mediators!

Review

➤ What happened during the session.

➤ What each of you did that was most and least helpful.

➤ What in retrospect you might have done differently.

➤ What you learned, what strategies you want to try in the future.

While your experience is fresh, write down any concerns, unusual problems, your breakthroughs, or other observations that will be helpful to other mediators.

SUPPORTING THE PEOPLE

Giving Good Attention

Acknowledging

Setting a Tone

Encouraging

Group Needs

Simple Language

Language and Hearing Difficulties

Confidentiality in Practice

Staying Impartial

Cultural Patterns

Emotionally
Difficult Situations

YOUR MEDIATOR'S TOOLBOX

❏ 3 KINDS OF TOOLS

The following three sections, Supporting the People, Controlling the Process, and Solving the Problem, are the trays in your giant "Mediator's Toolbox." Each is full of the tools that a mediator needs to handle each side of the Conflict Triangle. These sections are designed as a resource and for ongoing self-assessment; don't feel you have to take in everything at once.

Knowing your tools for each side of the triangle gives you a variety of options in any given moment. For example, if the parties start screaming at each other, you might try any of these responses:

Supportive mediator: *I can tell that you both care passionately about this issue, and you're both furious about what the other person has done. Now, I'm here to make sure you each get a fair deal without having to shout to be heard. No one is happy with the way things are. So let's take a deep breath here and see if we can sort things out. We'll start with something you mostly agree on…*

Process-control mediator: *Quiet! Thank you. Now, I need your commitment that there will be no more shouting. You've done that for several months now, and you're here because it doesn't work. Does everyone agree to that? Okay, let's go around again and give each of you another turn speaking with no interruptions. I want you to listen even if you don't like what you hear—and I promise you'll have a chance to respond.*

Problem-solving mediator: *Phew, this really is a hot issue, isn't it? Since this shouting clearly isn't getting you anywhere, let's step back and summarize what matters most to each of you, to make sure we've all understood. Then I suggest we take just one piece of it, the use of the cars, and brainstorm five or six different ways you might manage this so that both of you are satisfied.*

All of these strategies can work. Become conscious of which kind of strategy you are choosing and why. Is your first instinct to connect with people? To rein in the process? Or is it to get more information, more points of agreement? If you can, choose a co-mediator who complements your own style.

PEOPLE

PROCESS

PROBLEM

GIVING GOOD ATTENTION

❑ WHY GOOD ATTENTION IS ESSENTIAL

Giving good attention means listening and observing with minimal distraction by your own thoughts. Being respectfully attentive does *not* mean that you agree with the speaker. It means that you are focusing on what the person is saying, rather than on how you are going to respond.

Being attentive is essential for mediators; all other skills flow from this ability to be present in the moment. It helps you to grasp the important issues and the interpersonal dynamics of the situation quickly so that you are more likely to make wise and timely interventions. It builds rapport with the parties and encourages them to be forthcoming. Furthermore, good attention helps the speaker because it is easier to think through and articulate a point of view when you are not interrupted or challenged.

More subtly, giving good attention to each party creates an atmosphere which invites them to be attentive towards each other as well. Your ultimate goal is to have each person truly hear what the others are saying, to expand their own narrow sphere of attention outward to include the other people and perspectives.

❑ Points for the Mediator

First, quiet your own mind

Even though the mediator is not emotionally entangled in the situation, being attentive can be hard. The mediator must listen patiently to drawn-out stories and wait for those who speak haltingly. The parties may be disorganized, their remarks trivial, vague, or contradictory; some will wander far off the subject, others clam up and refuse to talk at all. Because conflict does not bring out the best in most people, you may find it difficult to listen to their mean, self-centered, or repetitious remarks.

If you want to set the stage for the possibility of transformation (rather than just a quick fix for the current problems), begin by putting aside your judgments, your ideas for solutions, your thoughts about where this mediation is going. And simply take in what they are telling you—verbally and non-verbally.

ELEMENTS OF GOOD ATTENTION

Your mind is focused. You notice both the emotion and the content the speaker is conveying, the interpersonal reactions, the context. You are not thinking about how to respond.

While you are listening, you put aside thoughts of what the person should do, who is right, what *you* would have done in that situation.

FOCUS

WITHHOLDING JUDGMENT

IMPARTIALITY & OPENNESS

CARING

Your face and posture show that you are listening. You look at others as well as the speaker to see how each person is reacting and to keep the participants from feeling that you are biased or gullible. You are careful that nods and murmurs do not make you appear to be agreeing with the speaker.

You are aware of the speaker as a person. You acknowledge the pain they have experienced in living with the conflict. You are interested in their concerns. Impartiality does not mean indifference.

ACKNOWLEDGING

❏ ACKNOWLEDGING

Acknowledging—simply letting people know they have been heard—is a skill which is at the core of good mediating, yet it is often underused. It tells the person that you have understood what they are trying to say without having to sympathize or react or judge or take action. Acknowledging allows the mediator to be respectful and attentive and still remain impartial.

Acknowledge their stories

For a surprising number of disputants, the chance to tell one's story and having someone else listen to it seriously means more to them than actually resolving the details of the situation.

> *From your point of view, this has been going on since the argument you had last February?*

> *So you've had a couple of incidents where no one explained to you what was happening and your daughter was really upset.*

Acknowledge their feelings

Often the "acting out" you see during a mediation melts away when people sense that you understand them. They stop trying to talk loudly or behaving rudely to get your attention. You can also lessen their embarrassment when you take their emotions as both serious and normal.

> *It sounds like you've been having a hard time for several years.*

> *So, what upsets you most is when people ignore you?*

Acknowledge their interests

For the same reasons, recognize out loud those things that matter most to each party. (See pages 94-5 and 114 for more ways to word this.)

> *Jean, this schedule may not affect you much, but it's clear that for Mary it is important because she feels her health is at stake.*

> *It sounds like you just don't want any more confrontations.*

> *I gather that for you, having a quiet street is most important; however, in order to get there we also need to talk about Ivan's concern about keeping his customers.*

© 1997 Friends Conflict Resolution Programs

SETTING A TONE

❏ SETTING A TONE

Tone is a subtle, yet vital, element of successful mediation. Essentially you are modeling the kind of attitude you hope the parties will have towards each other during and after the session.

Mediators try to create an atmosphere that encourages civil interactions and the courage to be honest. This means walking a fine line between friendly informality and formal seriousness of purpose. Setting the tone involves more than how you speak. It arises from a dozen details: how you dress, how you set up the room, whether you offer food, how you greet people, how you respond to outbursts.

Different mediations will need a different tone; moreover, each mediator creates a different atmosphere. Here are some elements which you may want to consciously foster:

▪ respect

    ▪ honesty

        ▪ confidence

           ▪ kindness

               ▪ attention

                  ▪ seriousness

                     ▪ friendliness

                        ▪ unhurried conversation

Perhaps the bottom line is recognizing each person as a person, not as a role or a case.

ENCOURAGING

❑ ENCOURAGING

A mediator's genuine confidence in the participants and in the mediation process—*You folks **can** resolve this, you have already made a lot of progress*—may give discouraged parties fresh momentum and help them tackle difficult, painful issues.

Encouraging doesn't mean being unrealistic or pressing people to be optimistic. It means being the outsider who gives voice to the hope and possibilities you can see that the participants may not.

Persuade, give them a sense of progress and of possibility, but go lightly with praise, as even genuine praise can easily sound condescending or surprised (as if you didn't expect them to behave well and they did).

➤ **Remind them of the positive steps they have taken.** At the very least they have come to the mediation table. Perhaps they have cleared up a misunderstanding, spoken forthrightly, offered new information, come to an agreement on one point, or listened thoughtfully. Notice!

You've both brought a lot of useful information to the table this morning—that's been helpful because I think everyone now has a better picture of the whole situation.

➤ **Give a progress report.** When you shift to a new phase or a new issue, summarize what they've accomplished so far and review the points they have already agreed to.

➤ **Convey your confidence that they can resolve the matter.**

Since that issue is critical for you, I think the others will be willing to add it to our agenda. Can I persuade you to bring it up at the table?

Yes, this is a difficult issue. I encourage you not to give up too soon—there may be several ways that you can retain your decision-making authority and still accommodate Bill's request for more autonomy.

You know, lots of mediations start out with yelling and hurt feelings and end up with agreements that actually hold. You've been very open, and if you hang in a bit longer, I think you will be able to resolve this so you don't have to live with it anymore.

➤ **Offer them your active support.**

Would you like me to bring the subject up first?

If she gets really angry again, I promise I'll step in right away.

GROUP NEEDS & SIMPLE LANGUAGE

❑ WATCHING GROUP AND INDIVIDUAL NEEDS

Watching out for the group's needs is not just a courtesy, as participants may find the mediation quite draining. Intervening when people are tired or strained is part of setting a hospitable tone and helps people concentrate on the task at hand.

Check that everyone can see and hear the rest of the group. Notice signs that attention is flagging, people start talking on the side, eyes glaze, or bodies get restless. The group might need a bit of light humor, a stretch break, an encouraging word, something to drink, a change of pace. Someone may need to talk about how they are feeling or a chance to retreat.

Checking in: How are you doing?

Whenever you aren't sure what someone needs or wants, ask them. Use a Separate Meeting if it is potentially touchy.

How is it going for you?

It's getting late. Should we break for the night?

You seem to be reacting strongly to what he said—are you okay?

❑ USING SIMPLE LANGUAGE

Better understanding. During a conflict and in an unfamiliar situation, people's ability to take in information is limited. Using simple language increases the ability of everyone to understand you. A simple summary after a confusing or complicated conversation can help everyone understand the discussion.

Demystifying mediation. Using a conversational style and avoiding specialized words from mediation, therapy, law, and other professions lessens the passive sense of "being mediated," of being a pawn in a process that seems mysterious and difficult to the uninitiated. Also, some people are less verbal or less educated; using ordinary conversational style helps welcome them as full participants.

LANGUAGE AND HEARING DIFFICULTIES

❑ LANGUAGE AND HEARING DIFFICULTIES

Here are some ways to include parties who, because of language or hearing, have trouble understanding or expressing themselves:

➢ The most important point: Remind yourself that people who have trouble understanding or speaking are more capable and mature than they appear to be.

➢ Allow extra time for each phase of the mediation. Take several breaks because it is hard to concentrate for long periods. Use this time to check in, to let the parties confer in their own language.

➢ Be vigilant about asking people to speak clearly and about keeping the pace from running away. This is easy to forget when discussion heats up or people are full of ideas.

➢ Try to be aware of how much the person is following the discussion.

➢ Give the person a longer time to compose a response, even if others are uncomfortable with longer silences.

➢ Keep your own language simple: short sentences, no idioms. Stress key words. Pause every sentence or two.

➢ Face the person when you speak but don't exaggerate your pronunciation. Gesture with your hands, use facial expressions.

➢ Use drawings, diagrams, write key words where all can see them.

➢ Give the person a draft copy as you read the agreement aloud.

Language

➢ If a mediator is bilingual, try to use both languages at the table. It may also be useful to write the agreement in both languages.

➢ Try to have associates or family members come to support the person, and select an uninvolved party to officially translate. Have a private conversation with the translator beforehand about roles and how you will work together. Translators often become interpreters and even de facto decision-makers. Try to communicate with the parties as directly as you can.

Difficulty reading

Some people do not read or write well and may be ashamed to admit this. (Or they may have forgotten their glasses!) Whenever you mediate, remember to routinely summarize aloud the content of any written materials and to read aloud the final agreement before asking people to sign.

AVOID THIS KETTLE OF FISH

CONFIDENTIALITY IN PRACTICE

❑ CONFIDENTIALITY

Maintaining confidentiality is one important way mediators support the people and the process. This includes what you say to others, what records you keep, and who has access to them. Remember that disputes can end up in court; weed out any non-essential information from your files. For sample policies, see pages 154-5.

Even if you are mediating informally, it is wise to be explicit with parties beforehand, during the opening, and again after the mediation about what you will or will not say to others. Note that you can only promise confidentiality for yourself; if the parties want to keep the proceedings private, that can be part of their agreement.

Confidentiality is not automatically a good thing. Private agreements are not always mindful of the public good. The privacy of a mediation session may prevent someone from receiving the kind of advice, information, benefits or rights that a public process might offer. It may be healthier for a whole organization or wider community to be at least informed about problems and proposals that will affect them, if not involved in making decisions about vital collective issues.

❑ CONFIDENTIALITY GUIDELINES

Here are some guidelines to consider in developing your own policy:

➢ Reveal any connections with the parties or potential conflicts of interest before the mediation begins.

➢ Destroy all but essential notes after the final session.

➢ Tell referral sources only whether a mediation was held and if so, whether an agreement was reached.

➢ Describe the mediation and participants to others in such a way that those familiar with the conflict will not recognize the identity of the parties. Do not use parties' names outside the session.

➢ Decide what you will do should a court subpoena you.

➢ Develop a clear policy about how you handle information that you cannot legally, professionally, or morally keep confidential, e.g., child abuse, danger of harm, some kinds of illegal activities.

➢ If a particular case would be useful for publication or research, ask the parties for written permission.

➢ Decline to mediate if you think the conflict, the negotiations, or the agreement should not be secret or exclusive.

STAYING IMPARTIAL

❑ IMPARTIALITY: PERCEPTIONS

When we asked disputants to comment on their mediators, the most frequent subject they raised was impartiality. They were particularly sensitive to whether the mediators "believed the lies" that the other side told. They tended to equate impartiality with feeling that the mediator sympathized with them.

The mediator has to think about impartiality from two divergent viewpoints:

➢ First, you want to facilitate fairly, without favoring any particular person or position. This means mentally setting aside your own biases, personal experiences, and judgments.

➢ Second, you need to monitor whether the parties *perceive* you as impartial, knowing that they may be desperate or suspicious enough to read all kinds of bias into your behavior that isn't there.

The first concern is between you and your conscience; the second can make or break the mediation.

Do the parties see me as impartial?

Appearances matter. Even if in your heart you know that you are impartial, if the parties think that you are biased, you will probably not be able to mediate effectively. Try to review your actions during and after the mediation with the question: "Is there any *chance* someone would see this as favoring the other side?"

Watch the participants for clues. Maybe they aren't looking at you; they seem to be fading out, pulling away from the table. Do they tend to address the other mediator? Do they argue often with what you say, question your credentials, or challenge your facilitating decisions?

Those disputants who expect you to be sympathetic and advocate on their behalf may never be satisfied, however they may respond positively when you talk openly about your need as mediator to be "fair to everyone" and not take sides. You can also remind them that what you think doesn't matter really; because they are going to have to live with their agreement; you will not.

> *I have a prejudice against disputants who come from different backgrounds, an underlying feeling of superiority. In one mediation—I felt pretty humble after that one—I was scornful of the women's speech.*
>
> *Then the other mediator said with warmth and love how much she respected them and gave them well-earned praise. It opened my eyes…You think you've reached a point where you are fair, that you are able to have a proper perspective but it is hard.*
>
> — a community mediator

STAYING IMPARTIAL

❑ WHAT'S IN YOUR MEDIATOR BAGGAGE?

How you affect the participants

As a mediator, you have authority. Even though you may not *want* the power to influence what the parties say and what they agree to, the reality is that your reactions may have a strong effect on the them.

How much of your "self" belongs in the mediation? The mediator's personality and presence is a vital part of the mediation, yet the minute the parties walk out the door you are no longer important. Keep your "self" in their present but out of their future.

You are most likely to step across that line when the parties make decisions that go against your own values and beliefs. Be particularly alert to class differences, which may be less conscious than other cultural, generational, racial, or gender differences. Here are some sticky areas:

- ➤ Child raising practices
- ➤ What being "professional" means
- ➤ What behavior is ethical
- ➤ How employees should behave / be treated

- ➤ How decisions should be made
- ➤ The importance of education
- ➤ Who deserves respect
- ➤ How organizations should run
- ➤ How loudly and rudely people should argue.

Of course these differences in matters of principle can also be major factors in the dispute. Learning to notice these underlying beliefs can help you to articulate and translate the parties' divergent perspectives.

STAYING IMPARTIAL

How the participants affect you

For each mediator, some people or issues are easier to mediate impartially than others. Take some time to notice what makes you most uncomfortable or irritable, and conversely, what kind of people or issues you tend to sympathize or identify with easily.

➤ Do you find yourself avoiding looking at someone or turning your body away?

➤ Are you cutting people off, or feeling annoyed when they speak?

➤ Does your facilitation highlight one side's issues and solutions?

➤ A common but subtle sign is using "you" to refer to a party you feel attuned to and "he" or "she" to refer to the others: *So, Jessica, you want the money back and Bob says he can't do that.*

➤ Do you find yourself trying to persuade someone to consider the other party's "reasonable" proposal or point of view?

If you aren't sure you are acting impartially, privately ask what your co-mediator thinks, and strategize together about how you can handle the situation.

❑ REMAINING IMPARTIAL

Naturally, you will have judgments, reactions, likes and dislikes. The question is, how do you put them aside while you are mediating? Some suggestions collected from our mediators:

➤ **Cultivate awareness:** Work at becoming more conscious of what your beliefs and principles are, knowing why some people "push your buttons" and exactly how you subtly communicate your reactions to others.

➤ **Be centered:** When you are centered, it is easier to separate their lives from yours. You have less desire to fix the parties' problems or to teach them something and a greater capacity to give them nonjudgmental attention.

➤ **Have a clear purpose:** A strong sense of why you are committed to doing mediations can help keep you on the path.

➤ **Empathize:** Find something in the irritating person or the situation that you like, that you find touching or encouraging, and focus on that aspect. Think of your job as bringing out the best in people who have seen each other at their worst.

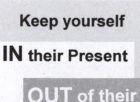

Keep yourself

IN their Present

OUT of their Future

CULTURAL PATTERNS

❑ CULTURAL DIFFERENCES IN MEDIATION

Most people take for granted the ways they learn to interpret and influence other people's behavior in a conflict. What does that person's silence mean? How should you argue? How should you negotiate or reconcile? Was that person's remark rude, friendly teasing, or a real threat? What is your responsibility in the situation?

Understanding these cultural patterns—both your own and the parties'—will help you adjust how you mediate to fit a particular dispute. At times you may need to talk about those differences at the table, acting as cultural interpreter between the parties.

Below we outline some contradictory cultural patterns that can affect a mediation. Of course in real life, no one adheres to just one interpretation or approach—we all vary our beliefs and responses according to the particular situation. For instance, how you speak to a family member when you are upset may not at all be the way you deal with an annoying customer or your dictatorial boss.

When you find a party's behavior puzzling or maddening, or when you are working with parties from a different culture, the categories and examples on the following pages may help you analyze what is happening and understand the role you need to play as mediator. Remember, you can often ask the parties directly to explain their thinking, their actions, and what they expect from the mediators.

❑ HOW SHOULD CONFLICT BE MEDIATED?

WHO	Impartiality is key to fair resolution; if the mediator is not connected to any of the parties, they are likely to trust the mediator more.
	Caring and involvement are important. The parties are more likely to trust a mediator they know and respect, someone who understands the nuances of the situation.
WHERE	Negotiations require privacy, getting away from outside pressures; a neutral location which favors neither party is preferable.
	Conflict resolution is most effective when it takes place in the location where the conflict occurs.
STRUCTURE	For serious negotiation, formal sessions work better. It helps to have distinct roles, explicit groundrules, and a clear process.
	People negotiate better in an informal environment that resembles social interaction between acquaintances.

CULTURAL PATTERNS

AUTHORITY / MEDIATOR ROLE	People should resolve their own problems. The mediator is there primarily as facilitator and referee. The mediators, as experts or elders, have experience in settling conflicts. They should take an active role in forming the solutions.
PROBLEMS / RELATIONS	The purpose of negotiation is problem solving; it is important to identify and discuss the key issues quickly. Naming problems too quickly is rude. It is more important to build a relationship first and work up to the touchy issues.
PROBLEM-SOLVING	Address one issue at a time. Deal with several aspects of the larger situation at once. Talk directly about some issues; skirt others. Talk or act in ways that signal your feelings/position and wait till the other side takes the hint.
THE BEST WAY TO RESOLVE CONFLICT	Decide who is at fault and determine appropriate restitution or punishment. A fair solution rights the balance. Precedent and rules are the basis for decisions. Everyone needs to give and take. Satisfy each party's interests. A good solution doesn't just solve the immediate problem, it takes away the underlying sources of friction. Change is good; creative new thinking will develop good solutions.
DESIRED OUTCOME	The parties may consider the conflict resolved when they: Restore balance. Strike a bargain. Achieve fairness or justice. Reach catharsis, listen to each other. Bridge the gap, clear up misunderstandings, open communication. Restore a relationship. Stop violence, attacks, friction. Solve their problems. Have their interests met. Are able to cooperate on future tasks.

CULTURAL PATTERNS

❑ HOW SHOULD PARTICIPANTS BEHAVE?

ROLE OF THE INDIVIDUAL	People should speak for themselves and be upfront about their needs and reactions. A good agreement takes into account the individual's needs, capabilities, and genuine assent.
	Whether or not people are negotiating for a constituency, their actions will have consequences for others in their group (family, department, association etc.), and their decisions should be based on that wider group's needs. Personal opinions and reactions are secondary.
ARGUING	Heated argument escalates conflict and shows that people are out of control. It also interferes with listening and with finding solutions.
	Heated argument is part of the truth-seeking process and helps bring out important issues. It shows how much people really care.
EMOTION & LEGITIMACY	Participants should put aside their emotional reactions so that negotiation can progress through calm and rational communication. Being civil, objective, controlled, and reasonable shows you have a legitimate position.
	Participants cannot be expected to let go of intense emotion until the negotiation shows some progress. Strong feelings are a sign of the legitimacy and importance of a concern.
SPEAKING	Speaking is the way to organize information and discussion. People should take turns speaking, get a fair share of "air time," and not interrupt others.
	Speaking is drama: the participants may tell stories, declaim, shout, talk over each other, gesture, stay silent or speak very quietly. The other side is convinced by evoking an emotional response in them.
SAVING FACE	Admitting that you have been wrong or backing down from a position can be unpleasant, but is appropriate in some circumstances.
	Admitting error or wrongdoing is deeply shameful, for you and maybe for your whole group.
	It is more considerate to go through a third party and not embarrass or anger someone by confronting them directly.
	It is more honest and mature to express your anger or criticism to someone directly than to go behind the person's back.

CULTURAL PATTERNS

❏ THE SAME ACTION = DIFFERENT MEANING

WHO IS GUILTY?	A person who remains silent when accused is probably guilty.
	A person who loudly defends him or herself is probably guilty.
	Apologizing means that you admit that the situation is your fault.
	Apologizing means you regret that the situation is causing pain or disruption, not that you are actually to blame. The other party is expected to respond with a parallel apology or a reassurance. ("That's okay, it's not really your fault.")
LISTENING	Nodding and saying "mm hmm," mean, "I agree with you."
	Nodding and saying "mm hmm," mean, "I am paying attention to you."
SILENCE	Silence is neutral or respectful. It means someone is not ready to speak or is deferring to someone else.
	Silence means you agree with what is said.
	Silence means you disapprove or have withdrawn from participating.
EYE CONTACT	Looking directly at the person you are talking with is polite and respectful. Looking away can mean evasion, deception, or disrespect.
	Looking directly at the person you are addressing may signal a challenge and can be seen as disrespectful.
THREATS	Threats mean a real intent to do harm and warn that the conflict is escalating to the boiling point.
	Threats are a way to let off steam without actually doing damage. They aren't meant literally.
QUESTIONS	Questions indicate interest and genuine concern.
	Questions are a form of attack; it is intrusive to ask someone to say more than they volunteer.
	Questions indicate the person is ignorant, or hasn't bothered to prepare for the negotiation.

EMOTIONALLY DIFFICULT SITUATIONS

❑ EXTREME ANGER

■ *I feel as if the mediation turned into an emotional hurricane of shouting and rage. Is there any hope for these people?*

First, ask yourself why they are showing anger right now.

➤ **Are they letting out a flood of pent-up, genuine emotion?** Ride it out as long as the other party is still attentive and not afraid or shouting back. If you think things might go too far, that they are out of control, interrupt the momentum by taking a break and giving the person a chance to cool off.

➤ **Is there something important this person desperately wants everyone to understand?** Restate the person's concern, reflecting their feelings and their perceptions. A little sympathy goes a long way. You may also ask the other party to summarize what they think the angry person wants them to understand.

➤ **Is the person attacking the other party?** Interrupt immediately. Acknowledge hot feelings. Get a verbal promise from everyone at the table that there will be no more attacks. You can do this at the table or in Separate Meeting.

➤ **Is the person deliberately trying to disrupt?** Remind yourself and them what the purpose of the session is and do not let angry outbursts deflect your commitment to a fair process that pays attention to everyone's needs.

❑ ANGUISH, CRYING

■ *Gwen is distraught and the rest of us are sitting at the table feeling embarrassed and not knowing what to say.*

➤ Take it in stride. Pass the tissue box. Sympathize in a general way: *Gwen, it is painful to listen to this, isn't it?* Show by your reactions that crying is a normal part of mediation sessions.

➤ If there has been a dramatic outburst, try to say very little. Your silence will press the others to recognize and speak to the person's pain. It can be a turning point.

➤ Ask Gwen if she would like to take a break, or just call one.

➤ Call a Separate Meeting to help the person regain control and, if necessary, to ask the other parties not to provoke.

➤ If Gwen wants to continue but doesn't want to be in the same room, try using shuttle diplomacy between separate rooms for a while.

© 1997 Friends Conflict Resolution Programs

EMOTIONALLY DIFFICULT SITUATIONS

❑ THE SILENT ONE

■ *Ever since Barbara lit into her, Julia has been sitting here with her arms folded and won't say a word. When we ask her questions or offer her a chance to speak, she just says, "I have nothing else to say."*

At the table

➢ State that this is everyone's session and everyone's agreement, so every person's point of view is needed. Acknowledge that it is difficult to talk when you are feeling upset or discouraged.

➢ Ask Barbara to make space for Julia to speak. Tell Julia that no one will interrupt her while she says what she has to say. Then wait expectantly for her to say something.

➢ Wait a longer time for a response than you usually might.

➢ Announce a second round of Uninterrupted Time if the other people present have said volumes more.

In Separate Meetings

➢ Reassure Julia that the conversation is confidential. Ask whether she has anything to tell you in private.

➢ Tell her what you observed: *You haven't been saying very much.*

➢ Ask if she can tell you what is making her uncomfortable.

It looks like you're really upset. Can you tell me what's going on? Is there anything I can do to make it easier for you to take part?

➢ If she still does not open up, point out the consequences of staying silent.

I'm not going to let Barbara dictate the terms of the agreement. If you don't want to work towards an agreement, then I need to end the mediation soon and you'll be back at Square One again. What do you want to do?

➢ With Barbara, explore ways she can help make it easier for Julia to speak her mind.

EMOTIONALLY DIFFICULT SITUATIONS

❏ PERSON WHO COMES IN BAD FAITH

■ *We both suspect that Mr. Berg has no intention of reaching a settlement.*

➢ Protect the other parties by being careful not to ask for information or give opinions that might become future fodder in a courtroom or escalate the anger level between parties.

➢ Don't waste your time trying to cajole Mr. Berg into participating.

➢ Try, in this order: meeting with him separately, addressing the problem at the table, discontinuing the mediation.

➢ Be direct with Mr. Berg about what you have observed. *Twice the Roseworks company has agreed to your requests, yet both times you have rejected their offer and made stronger demands.*

➢ Ask whether he is here to resolve the situation and willing to participate in working towards a resolution. Get a verbal answer.

➢ Encourage him to be honest. *If you don't want to continue with this, please say so. No one is required to be here or to reach an agreement.*

➢ Ask if there is anything you can do to make the mediation work better for him.

➢ Review Mr. Berg's options with him: *What will happen if you leave this mediation now?*

➢ When you sense that he is not interested in working towards an agreement, don't clutch at him with persuasive arguments. Let him go.

CONTROLLING THE PROCESS

Directing

Should I Intervene?

Setting Boundaries & Groundrules

Summarizing

Restating

Confronting

Protecting

Is it Time to Quit?

When Things Get Out of Control

❑ DIRECTING THE SESSION

Directing is tricky because you want them to have ownership—this is *their* mediation. Nevertheless, they are relying on you for structure and for protection. Directing the flow of a session requires many skills. It also demands unflagging attention as you tune into a number of channels at once.

The following pages lay out directing skills for routine facilitating, followed by controlling skills for when the waters get rough.

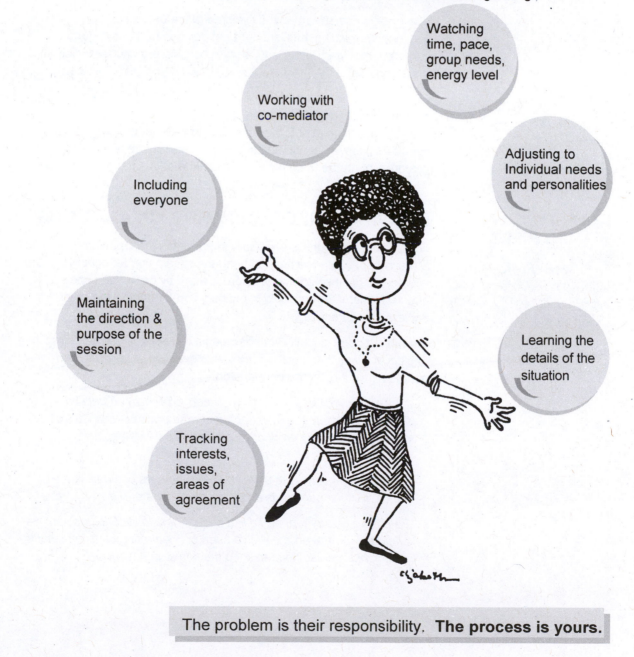

Watching time, pace, group needs, energy level

Working with co-mediator

Adjusting to Individual needs and personalities

Including everyone

Learning the details of the situation

Maintaining the direction & purpose of the session

Tracking interests, issues, areas of agreement

The problem is their responsibility. **The process is yours.**

DIRECTING

❑ SETTING A TONE

In the Opening Statement and Supporting the People sections, we discussed setting a tone. The atmosphere you create at the mediation session is also a valuable tool for keeping control of the process. Your tone signals that you are at ease and in control, and quietly shows that you expect civil behavior.

Be conscious of your presence: how does your manner convey what kind of behavior and attitudes you expect from the parties?

Use your voice effectively: Develop a range of voices— warm and gentle, commanding, efficient "let's get down to business," good-humored, matter-of-fact— and learn to consciously choose which voice you use.

Be aware of the non-verbal messages you send. Keep your posture and gaze open, unworried, and alert. Try to equalize the time you spend looking at or tilting your body towards each party. When you need to assertively control the session, let your expressions and gestures mirror the forcefulness of your words.

❑ GIVING DIRECTIONS AND EXPLANATIONS

> ### CONNECT
>
> Before you say something important, look around the table and get *each person's* attention.
>
> Keep that connection while you are speaking.

Giving clear directions is especially important in the Opening Statement or when you need to bring the session under control. Before you speak, get their attention. Address them by name, and speak directly to them as you would in ordinary conversation. Use short, declarative sentences.

You do not need to justify your decisions. However, if you can direct or explain in a way that highlights how your decision will benefit them, that can help gain their active cooperation.

That's enough! Greg, Lonnie, you need to be hold off until I am finished speaking. (Look at each man and pause.) *Now, let's use our time here today productively. Here's how we're going to proceed…*

Sarah, Wright, let's take a break now. I think we could all use a minute to clear our heads and think about where to go from here

Before we go any further, I'd like each of you to list 3 things you like about the current policy. We've been concentrating on fixing what's wrong, but we also need to keep the things that work well.

DIRECTING

❏ BALANCING PARTICIPATION

Balancing participation can require both persistence and tact.

➤ Tell them how you want them to participate, and why.

In mediation each person speaks for themselves, even kids.

This morning it will be just as important to listen as to talk.

➤ Intervene when a party dominates the airwaves without making them feel like their contributions are unwelcome.

Let's let James finish and then you can respond. (Raise your hand slightly in a restraining gesture to reinforce your words.)

Can you hold it there and let Lynn have a chance to explain?

➤ Coax quiet parties into speaking. In general, focus on getting each person to join in, rather than on restraining the more vocal participants.

Latisha, we haven't heard what you think about this yet.

❏ INTERRUPTING

Here are several strategies for interrupting, from gentle to forceful:

➤ Acknowledge that you are interrupting. *Excuse me for interrupting you, Herb, but I think this is getting off the subject.* Notice that the mediator is firm but also avoids accusing or ordering.

➤ Use people's names, look at them directly.

➤ Gesture cutting into the conversation or give the Time Out signal

➤ Speak louder.

➤ Use a few, abrupt, commanding words (not a stream of words).

➤ Slap your hand or notepad on the table.

➤ Stand up, lean forward, put your arms out.

When you have broken through, pause to hold their attention before you speak. Then lower your voice. The pivotal moment is often these few seconds *after* you have succeeded in interrupting and they are momentarily silent. Be immediately directive to keep them from plunging in again: change the mood or the subject, insist they change their behavior, take a break.

SHOULD I INTERVENE?

❑ SHOULD I INTERVENE?

The discussion has gone off on a tangent.

The parties are speaking rapidly in raised voices, cutting each other off and calling each other names.

The parties are speaking deliberately and without a trace of emotion, careful to be coolly objective in everything they say.

Everyone is talking at once.

One party tells long, detailed stories about what happened.

The Exchange has become painfully emotional.

Any of these conversations may be productive or they may indicate a downward spiral that needs intervention. Just because the parties seem loud or rude or upset or they are talking at the same time doesn't mean that they aren't getting anywhere. How do you tell?

Let it continue	Intervene
▫ The participants are saying new things, exchanging new information.	▪ Someone seems intimidated.
▫ The participants seem to accept the emotional level of the discussion.	▪ The participants are repeating themselves.
▫ Everyone seems to be holding their own in the discussion.	▪ They are getting increasingly polarized and rigid in their positions.
▫ The parties are hearing and responding to each other.	▪ Accusations seem to be aimed at hurting rather than expressing or discussing.
▫ The subject of discussion seems important to the disputants even if it seems irrelevant or off the track to you.	▪ The participants have gotten sidetracked onto unhelpful topics.
▫ You sense that the parties are approaching an emotional turning point.	▪ Some people are not listening.
	▪ The parties seem unable to move from namecalling and personal attacks to talking about the issues.

SETTING BOUNDARIES & GROUNDRULES

❑ SETTING BOUNDARIES

Part of controlling the process is deciding and enforcing the limits of what the session can cover and what behavior is acceptable. As with the decision to intervene, try to make the judgment on the basis of what will bring these people to a resolution, rather than on what makes *you* personally uncomfortable.

You may have to:

➢ **Limit the issues discussed.** What gets discussed now, what will be handled later, and what is off limits? This is best decided with the parties' input.

➢ **Establish the mediator's role.** Some disputants will try to control the mediation by drowning out other voices, trying to take over as facilitator, or by challenging the mediators' directions. Maintain your control of process decisions.

I know you want to discuss B, and we'll get there. We need to deal with A first. Can I have your agreement on that?

If this doesn't work, confront the person in a Separate Meeting.

➢ **Set groundrules for appropriate behavior.**

❑ SETTING GROUNDRULES

As we mentioned earlier, our preference is *not* to state groundrules in the beginning. You do not want to imply that the parties may not "behave" or that you are worried about keeping control. Most importantly, this lets the parties get credit for being civil or respectful, rather than for just obediently following your rules.

That said, groundrules can be very useful because everyone hears what behavior is appropriate and expected.

Raise your concern about how the parties are interacting and help them come to agreement on how they will proceed.

There seem to be several side conversations going on. Is that okay with everyone? Should we ask people to call a break when they need to confer?

Sometimes it is wiser to simply invoke a groundrule without discussion:

Excuse me. In mediation we have a groundrule of no namecalling. Do I have your agreement on that?

Before moving on, be sure you get verbal agreement or a clear nod from each person.

SUMMARIZING

When you don't know what to say…

SUMMARIZE

❑ SUMMARIZING: WHERE ARE WE?

Summarizing is the mediator's trusty multi-purpose flashlight, helping to keep the session on track. It gives voice and shape to those things that are most important. Mediators summarize to focus the group's attention and to help everyone understand and organize the different threads and layers of their discussion.

Summarizing is a difficult skill. You are distilling the essence of what is important from a discussion while giving people direction and impetus to keep going. This requires close attention to what is happening. Summarizing needs to be succinct and at times calls for impromptu eloquence. Fortunately, if you are inarticulate the first time, all is not lost; just try again a few minutes later.

Reasons to summarize

➢ **Reinforce the progress they've made.**

You're making headway here. You've cleared up a few important personal issues. And here are the points of agreement so far…

➢ **Identify their concerns.** This is especially helpful during the Exchange, before they are ready for a structured agenda.

Let's see where we are. Trina is talking about caseload, and Johann is bringing up lots of budget issues. Each of you is concerned about very different aspects of the situation.

➢ **Point out mutual interests or areas of agreement.**

Clearly you both want to be involved in this project and you both care about getting public credit for the work you've done.

➢ **Organize information: what the group knows, doesn't know.**

We've heard about how this has affected the children—being afraid to ride the bus, namecalling, some stone throwing—but we haven't yet heard how the situation is affecting the parents.

➢ **Tie up loose ends and move to another topic.**

We've covered most of the security issues and heard Nancy's report. (Review decisions briefly.) We still have to cover the supervision issues, and how you will handle future problems.

➢ **Review areas of disagreement, work left to do.**

Okay, so we're still left with the property line issue. And with questions about both the easement and the surveyor's report.

RESTATING

❑ RESTATING FOR THE MEDIATOR

Restating means summarizing in your own words what someone has said. In just a few economical phrases, restating allows you to doublecheck your own understanding, let the parties know that you heard them, and help one party take in what the other is saying.

You can restate concerns, proposals, perspectives, or information.

> *Ella, as I understand it, your main concern is getting fair reimbursement for the damage to your windows. And you've been frustrated by the interactions you and Sam have had so far, is that right?*

> *Sam, you are reluctant to pay because you don't think it was your fault. You'd like to see this situation over and done with. Is there something I missed?*

Caution: Take care not to sound as if you are advocating or approving. Notice that the mediator addresses the person: *Sam, you are…*, rather than describing Sam's position to the table: *I think Sam is reluctant to pay because…* Use the latter only if you are sure neither party will think you are agreeing with Sam.

KEEP IT SIMPLE
➢ State key elements of what the person said.
➢ Omit details, explanations.
➢ Keep your own opinion from coloring your words.
➢ Check that you got it right.

❑ ASKING THE PARTICIPANTS TO RESTATE

Are people talking past each other? Not responding to important points the other has raised? Ignoring significant concessions, agreements, or acknowledgments the other party has offered?

Asking one party to restate what another person has said can help everyone listen and acknowledge what the issues and feelings are.

Couple the request with an opportunity for the speaker to comment so that the speaker doesn't feel forced to give credence to the other party's distasteful words.

> *Alex, would you summarize what Florence just said, and then give us your response?… Florence, is that what you meant?*

Be sure you are evenhanded. Ask for restating from both sides.

Use this strategy *cautiously*, as parties can easily feel patronized or coerced, especially during the early phases of mediation when they are not emotionally ready to acknowledge the other parties' point of view.

CONFRONTING

❏ CONFRONTING THE PARTICIPANTS

Sometimes mediators need to confront disputants who are disrupting the mediation or verbally attacking the other party. This can happen at the table or in a Separate Meeting.

➢ Describe their behavior, its effect on the mediation, and other possible consequences.

You have interrupted Marjorie many times, even when I asked you to stop. If she walks out, she may go talk to the newspaper again. You said you don't want that to happen.

➢ Be assertive, not tentative. Sound like you mean it.

➢ Remember your Supporting skills: Assume that they intend to behave well. Acknowledge their feelings and point of view. Help them save face by using Separate Meetings.

I know it is difficult to listen to her say things you think are lies.

➢ Speak to their interests when you are trying to convince them to change their behavior.

Are you serious about wanting to keep this job? Then you need to figure out how you can work together even if you don't like her.

➢ Tell them explicitly what you want them to do.

That means letting her have a chance to finish what she's saying, and holding back from attacking her character.

➢ Get a commitment before returning to the discussion.

Are you willing to do that?

❏ EXPLORING CONSEQUENCES

If a party persists in disrupting and attacking, or wants to leave, explore with them in a Separate Meeting what effect their choice would have on (to pick a few): their future interactions with the other party, their reputation, getting what they say they want, the level of conflict (and aggravation), their bargaining power, court suits, their ability to do their job, their physical safety.

The mediator's job is to help the person understand the possible consequences of their behavior. However, our model of mediation is voluntary. Ultimately, if people want to be stubborn, rude, foolish, to quit the session or take their problem elsewhere, that is their choice. End the session if they are not willing or able to follow the groundrules.

PROTECTING

❑ PROTECTING THE PARTIES

The mediator is responsible for the safety of the mediation session. In our experience, it is rare that anyone tries to physically attack the other party during a mediation, but threats and verbal attacks are common.

Psychological protection

For some disputants, being in the same room with someone they consider an enemy can be intimidating or frightening. Here again, the tone you set of easy, confident control can be reassuring, as can acknowledging their nervousness.

> *I know it's not comfortable to be in the same room with each other. Thank you for agreeing to come under these difficult circumstances.*

Use a table, seat them at a distance. And of course, intervene quickly if you sense that someone cannot cope with the hurtful things the other party is saying.

Privacy protection

You may also need to shield people from prying questions or off-limits topics. If they are concerned about keeping the dispute confidential, the parties can put a confidentiality clause in their agreement detailing what they can report about today's session and to whom. (See pages on Confidentiality, page 76.)

Physical protection

Protecting the parties and the mediators' physical security means preparing carefully before a mediation. (See sidebar.)

If physical protection is a significant concern, face-to-face mediation is probably not appropriate unless you are doing ongoing intervention and know the parties well. Even if you have a safe place to hold the mediation, you may put someone at risk after the mediation if an aggressive party is not happy with the outcome.

If information emerges during a mediation which gives you concern about someone's safety and the parties are not close to reaching agreement, end the session. You may want to see that each party gets to their car. If they can reach real agreement, that may help defuse the situation. Even so, you may want to give out contact numbers to a party after the session in case they experience more trouble.

IS IT TIME TO QUIT?

❏ IS IT TIME TO QUIT?

There are times when a wise mediator ends a mediation session. Ask yourself these two questions:

1. Can they negotiate fairly and usefully?

Here are several warning flags:

➢ A key person seems incapable of participating productively:

- The person persists in threatening or disrupting

- The person keeps repeating accusations and demands, even when the group has already agreed to accommodate them

- No amount of explanation resolves a person's confusion.

➢ A fair agreement is unlikely. For instance, the power differential may mean that one side is caving in to the other's demands.

➢ The main problems are not negotiable.

➢ A party who is a critical part of the dispute is absent. Or the person representing a group has not been authorized to make commitments.

2. Does mediating potentially endanger someone?

Occasionally, there are conflicts where a face-to-face negotiation session can be unfair or even dangerous for participants, other potential victims, for the organization, or for the community. You should stop the mediation if you have good reason to believe that:

➢ One party might react with violence, vengeance, or intimidation after the mediation.

➢ One party is covertly using mediation to elicit information that will be used against the other party (in court, to fire them, etc.) or as an opportunity for retaliation.

➢ Someone is using mediation as a way to keep illegal or unethical behavior under cover. By mediating, a person can avoid getting an official record or punishment. They don't have to admit fault in public. There may be future victims because a confidential mediation makes it harder to establish that there is a pattern of incidents going on.

➢ The agreement they are proposing is illegal or is harmful to people who aren't represented at the mediation.

© 1997 Friends Conflict Resolution Programs

IS IT TIME TO QUIT?

❑ BREAKING OFF THE MEDIATION

Usually the parties break off the mediation before the mediators are ready to give up. When the mediator initiates, it can be hard to know when and how to draw the line. Consult with your co-mediator first and give yourselves a chance to think through what to do. It can be difficult to determine what is really going on and you will have to rely on your intuition.

Be sensitive to participants' interpretations of why you are ending a mediation. For instance, don't end the mediation abruptly following a separate meeting or one party's outburst, leaving others to imagine what was said privately, or that the mediator disapproved of one party's point of view.

Try to remain impartial as you withdraw from the mediation. (Remember too, that no matter how much they tell you, you are getting an incomplete and skewed picture from the participants.)

Try to end the session without blaming or discouraging the participants. You don't need to be explicit about the reasons, either.

> *I don't think we can get any further right now. I'm glad you were able to (have an honest discussion, reach agreement on X, give mediation a try).*

> *Thank you all for coming. I don't think this is the right place for you to discuss this situation. If you would like some assistance on where to turn next, I'd be happy to meet with each of you privately for a few minutes now before you leave.*

If you have information or concerns to convey, meet with each party separately at the end, or call them the following day.

You will want to evaluate in detail afterwards, of course, but don't be hard on yourselves. A good mediator knows the limits of what they can deal with in a mediation process.

WHEN THINGS GET OUT OF CONTROL

❑ OUT OF CONTROL

■ *The participants are all screaming at each other, and we've tried every interrupting and calming tactic in the book.*

■ *The man whose kid was hurt got up and shook his finger right in the other guy's face. What should I do—go stand between them?*

1. **Stand up.** Insist on getting their attention. Stand near the person who is most out of control. Call people by their names, try to get them to look at you. Speak in command sentences: *Victor, you must sit down!* If this only riles them further, you can ask the less agitated party to step out of the room for a minute to help diffuse the situation.

2. **Appear calm, decisive, and in charge.** If you are worried or uncertain, don't show it.

3. **Keep close contact with your co-mediator.**

4. **Call for a break immediately.**

5. **Confront.** In Separate Meetings, use the confronting sequence:

   ▪ Describe their behavior.

   ▪ Talk about consequences of their behavior, including ending the mediation.

   ▪ Tell them what you want them to do.

   ▪ Get a verbal commitment.

   Remember that a quiet, supportive approach works with some people, a blunt approach with others.

7. **Think about what they gain.** Try to figure out what they gain by the uproar. Are they disrupting because they have no intention of participating? Are they too upset to control themselves ? Do they seem to enjoy it? Are they trying to convince others how angry they are? Trying to intimidate you or the other party? You may want to raise these questions with them directly once things calm down.

8. **Set boundaries and stick to them.** Tell them plainly that you will stop the session if they repeat the previous behavior again. Then carry through with it.

© 1997 Friends Conflict Resolution Programs

WHEN THINGS GET OUT OF CONTROL

❏ I'M OUTTA HERE

■ *Jacquie announced, "I'm outta here," and stalked out of the room. Now the Whites are saying, "Well, that's it, we're leaving too."*

One mediator should follow Jacquie and ask to talk with her privately before she decides to leave. The other mediator will talk with the Whites.

➢ Hear the parties out, acknowledge their frustrations. If you can get them talking for a while, they will probably agree to continue with the mediation.

➢ Ask Jacquie what you can do to make it possible for her to come back in and try again.

➢ Discuss the potential consequences of breaking off the mediation, but don't imply that you are desperate to have them stay. If they want to break it off, that is their choice.

❏ DISTURBED PEOPLE

■ *Andrew seems paranoid about everything and everybody. There's no way he trusts anyone enough to make an agreement.*

■ *Joyce has been in a rage most of the session, except when she starts to sob. Nothing anyone says has made the slightest dent.*

➢ If the person has come with others, they may be helpful as intermediaries. Give them time to calm the person and to explain. Otherwise, give yourself lots of time to fill that function.

➢ Maintain a quiet tone.

➢ Often the other party understands the difficulty. During a Separate Meeting, talk to them about how to get through or at least not trigger a reaction. *I can understand why it is hard to discuss this problem with Joyce. Let's think of how you can lessen her anxiety.*

➢ Let the other participants reach an agreement. The troubled person can sign or not, but be frank with the others present that upholding the agreement is going to be mostly their task.

WHEN THINGS GET OUT OF CONTROL

❑ ATTACKING THE MEDIATORS

■ *All of a sudden, Henry lights into us, saying we are prejudiced against him. "You are nice ladies, but Thomas is just using you." I was so surprised, I didn't know what to say.*

When someone accuses you of bias or challenges the way you are facilitating the session:

➢ Ask what you did specifically that concerns the person.

➢ Do not try to disagree, just thank them for the honest input.

➢ If they are even partly right, apologize. Agree on what you will do differently from now on.

➢ Otherwise, interpret their behavior as *resistance*—to the process, to facing an uncomfortable truth, to reaching agreement.

➢ Ask them for another half hour of their time. Say that if they are still dissatisfied at that point, then you will end the session.

➢ Follow their resistance to learn more about their interests:

Are you worried that everyone believes Mr. Thomas and not you?

Are you concerned about being used in this situation?

You seem reluctant to continue.

Taking Notes

Asking the Right Questions

Negotiation Terms

Interests

Positions

Mediatable Issues

Reframing Their Words

Eliciting Ideas

Exploring Alternatives

Testing for Agreement

Sample Agreements

When No Resolution is in Sight

TAKING NOTES: WHAT TO LISTEN FOR

Names of the parties

Interests
➤ What seems to be most important to each person?

Values
➤ Note differences *and* ones they share

Issues that can be mediated
➤ This will become your Issue Checklist

Ideas and suggestions raised

Sticking Points
➤ Need more information
➤ Issues to address in another session
➤ Issues to refer to another forum

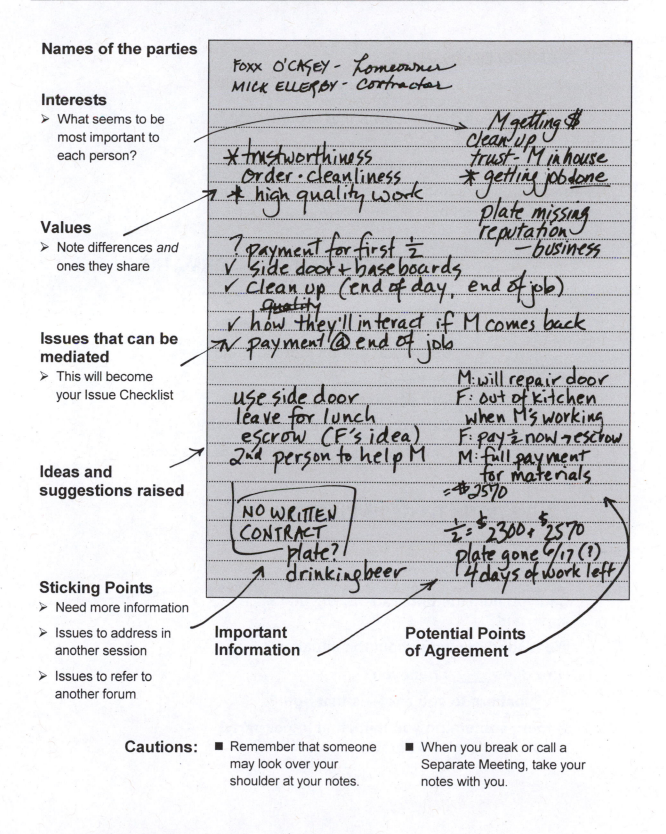

FOXX O'CASEY - homeowner
MICK ELLERBY - contractor

M getting $
clean up
trust - M in house
*getting job done

*trustworthiness
order · cleanliness
* high quality work

plate missing
reputation
— business

? payment for first ½
✓ side door + baseboards
✓ clean up (end of day, end of job)
  quality
✓ how they'll interact if M comes back
✓ payment @ end of job

use side door
leave for lunch
escrow (F's idea)
2nd person to help M

M: will repair door
F: out of kitchen
   when M's working
F: pay ½ now → escrow
M: full payment
   for materials
   = $2570

NO WRITTEN
CONTRACT
  plate?
  drinking beer

½ = $2300 + $2570
plate gone 6/17 (?)
4 days of work left

Important Information

Potential Points of Agreement

Cautions:
- Remember that someone may look over your shoulder at your notes.
- When you break or call a Separate Meeting, take your notes with you.

??? ASKING THE RIGHT QUESTIONS ¿¿¿

❑ OPENING QUESTIONS

…use these questions when you begin the Uninterrupted Time

Could you tell us the concerns that brought you here today?

Please explain to us what has been happening.

Can you give us some background?—tell us your view of the situation.

❑ QUESTIONS TO GET INFORMATION

… use these questions during the Exchange

Can you give me an example?

Could you tell me more about how you view _____?

Can you explain _____?

Can you help me understand why _____?

Could you describe what happened when _____?

❑ QUESTIONS TO GET AT INTERESTS

… use these questions during the Exchange

What is important to you?

Can you help me understand *why* that's important?

What concerns you about the situation?

How does _____ affect you?

_____ matters to you a lot—is that right?

Is there something you think that [other party] doesn't understand about your situation?

??? ASKING THE RIGHT QUESTIONS ¿¿¿

❏ QUESTIONS TO GET AT SOLUTIONS

… use these questions when you are working on specific issues during Building the Agreement

What might work for you?

What can *you* do to help resolve this issue?

What other things might you try?

What would make this idea work better for you?

Is there some way we can meet both X's need for _____ and Y's need for _____?

❏ QUESTIONS TO GET AT CONSEQUENCES

… use these questions during the Exchange and again during Building the Agreement

What other options do you have if you don't reach agreement today?

Are you planning to move? (get another job. . . .)

What problems might there be with this idea?

If you agree to this solution and _____ happens, then what?

❏ QUESTIONS TO TEST AGREEMENT

… use these questions during Building and Writing the Agreement

Is this agreement acceptable to everybody?

Have we covered everything?

Is there any piece of this you're uneasy with?

Now, is this what you're agreeing to: _____ ?

Can you live with this every day, every week from now on?

??? ASKING THE RIGHT QUESTIONS ¿¿¿

❑ ASK YOUR QUESTIONS WITH CARE

A good question helps everyone—the disputants *and* the mediators—understand what the issues are. Asking questions also directs a discussion. If the conversation is foundering, a well-placed question can get people going. Otherwise, try not to overly control the direction of discussion with your questions. Do you or the other party really need to know certain information? If not, don't ask.

Eliciting different types of information

➢ **Description.** *What happens when you and Sheila try to talk?*

➢ **Facts.** *How often does your board meet?*

➢ **Feelings and perspectives.** *What concerns you about her actions? How do you feel about what was just said?*

➢ **New thinking.** *Who might be able to help you with that?*

Eliciting different types of replies

Open-ended questions allow many different replies. Use them to draw people out, to get an overview, to let the speaker direct what is discussed.

> *What does a typical day look like?*

> *What happened last week that upset you?*

Directive questions invite a short answer. Ask talkative or dominant people questions which focus their attention on specific topics or require a clear, short answer. Use direct questions to pin down specific information or contain a long-winded speaker.

> *What time do you usually leave work?*

> *Did this happen after you got the letter?*

Leading questions suggest the mediator approves of a particular answer. In general, mediators *avoid* leading questions such as:

> ✗ *Wouldn't it be better to get the property surveyed first?*

> ✗ *What would happen if you talked more calmly to Jay?*

"What" questions. When you can, substitute "what" for "why." Instead of saying: *Why don't you respond?*, ask: *What makes it hard for you to respond to Jim's requests?* "Why" questions tend to make people defensive and can be hard to answer. "What" asks for specific, descriptive replies.

NEGOTIATION TERMS

The next pages review several negotiation terms: interests, positions, and issues. Mediators use these concepts to organize the information they hear and to structure problem-solving so that the topic and goals of the discussion are clear and the parties are able to move away from fixed positions.

Problem	Interpretation	Position	Interest	Issue
The immediate source of conflict	How people interpret the other party's behavior	Demands, threats, fixed solutions, proposals, or points of view	What really matters to this person. (*Why* is X a problem?)	The topic the parties need to discuss and decide.
Barking dog.	Neighbor is unfriendly, inconsiderate. Violates my privacy.	Buy a muzzle.	I'm not well. I need my sleep. Want my home to be a quiet, private place.	How to control the barking at night.
Unfair bill.	This company wants to rip me off. They think I'm not smart enough to notice.	I will not pay for work you didn't even do.	Want to be treated fairly. Need to know how much something is going to cost so I can budget for it.	What work was done, what recompense is fair. How rest of job will be billed.
Rude treatment, exclusion from meetings.	This guy is a snake. He's undermining me in front of my boss.	You owe me an apology.	Keeping up a good reputation. Less stress at work.	Who attends meetings. How people speak to each other.
Tenant owes me 3 months back rent.	Tenant is a freeloader. Tenant may go bankrupt.	Pay $800 this month or I'll evict you.	Fairness. Getting the money. Reliable rental income.	Payment plan. Repair plan.

INTERESTS

☐ INTERESTS: WHAT MATTERS AND WHY

As we discussed earlier, a conflict occurs when people believe that something important to them is threatened. In negotiations, those important concerns are called "interests." The term is broad. All of these might be interests, for example: financial wellbeing, saving face, fair work rules, living up to one's principles, a closer relationship, maintaining privacy, retaining control, personal safety, and regaining one's health.

Listening for their interests

Understanding people's interests is not a simple task. The mediator can hypothesize about what is important to each party but one can never be sure what is in the mind and heart of another person, especially if the mediator is meeting the disputants for the first time.

Listen for these cues about interests:

➢ **What matters to each person:** practically, emotionally, and socially.

➢ **What they most hope to resolve.**

➢ **The effect the problem has** on their daily life and on their spirit. If they are living in suspicion and anger, if they have varied their routine so as not to encounter the person, if they have built fences or arranged to transfer jobs… the mediator knows that something very important to the person is being threatened. Try to find out what they are afraid will happen.

➢ **What issues are particularly hot.**

➢ **Any common underlying themes** connecting several issues. For instance, perhaps every issue that one party brings up relates to the larger question of who controls how the group's money is spent. Or you may sense that hurt feelings over being excluded seem to fuel the person's indignation more than the particulars of the incidents and issues involved.

➢ **The golden nugget*:** Can you find some positive, caring, generous self amid the complaints, self-centeredness, and blame? (A classic example is when a parent spanks a child who has just narrowly missed getting hit by a car. The golden nugget is the loving desire to protect their child from harm.)

* *This concept comes from the work of Ricky Sherover-Marcuse.*

QUESTIONS TO GET AT INTERESTS

What is important to you?

What bothers you about the situation?

How does _____ affect you?

It sounds like _____ matters to you a lot—is that right?

INTERESTS

❏ INTERESTS MAY HAVE SEVERAL LAYERS

In a dispute, people may state that they have one and only one concern. It is rare that in fact only one thing matters to them, however; more likely they have several layers of interests at stake.

For example, say a couple is fighting about whether to vacation in the mountains or at the ocean…

At first you may take their argument at face value and think that Susan loves being in the mountains, while Bob prefers beaches.

⇩

Then you may find out that she really loves to hike, which is she can't do at the beach, while he just wants to relax someplace warm and do nothing.

⇩

Digging deeper, you may discover that Sue is interested in winning this argument because she gave in to Bob the last two years. Or maybe he wants them to have time alone and going to the mountains means visiting her family.

⇩

And some interests are so private, the mediators can only guess at them.

All of these levels are interests. All may be simultaneously true. The question for mediators is which interests matter the most to the parties? Which ones can mediation address? Which ones will help the next step in resolving this conflict?

Different kinds of intervention (see pages 134-5) focus on different layers of interests. Authorities, such as the police and courts, and sometimes supervisors or parents, tend to focus on the outer layers, the immediate and visible interests. At the other end of the spectrum, therapists and ministers help people in conflict look at the core interests: a person's underlying psychological and spiritual needs.

Mediators work in the middle layers. They concentrate on interests which may be deeply personal but which also intersect with the outside world because the dispute also involves things, tasks, and other people.

INTERESTS

HAVING DIFFICULTIES WITH SOMEONE?

➢ *People:* If you need to persuade or encourage…

➢ *Process:* If the session gets out of control …

➢ *Problem:* If they're having trouble coming to agreement …

Speak to the person's interests

❏ WHICH INTERESTS MATTER?

Mediators will not have time to assess all the layers of a party's interests. Besides, the parties have not asked the mediator to delve into their psyches (and if they did, the mediator would, of course, decline). Instead the mediator needs to be thorough *enough* to discover:

➢ **Interests that seem genuine.** Interests professed during Uninterrupted Time may be more for public presentation of self than an expression of what really matters to that person.

➢ **Interests that can realistically be discussed and satisfied**.

➢ **Interests that draw them to commit to the mediation and to the agreement.**

➢ **Interests that are sufficiently important** to the parties that if met, the dispute will probably diminish or end.

❏ THE MEDIATOR'S MANTRA

They're not listening. They're uncooperative. They have a one-track focus. They are acting out. They're walking out the door…. Any time you need to reach someone, invoke the mediator's mantra to yourself:

Speak to the person's interests

—not to what *you* think is in their best interest, but what that person seems to think and feel is important. People are more likely to take your requests and suggestions seriously if they see a benefit for themselves.

> *I understand that you are concerned about your safety. What specific things can Lynne do which would make you feel safer?*

> *You want her to just leave you alone—yes? Here's how mediation can help you get there… For that to happen, I need your commitment to speak only for yourself, as we agreed, and to hold back on the namecalling. That way we can finish here tonight, and hopefully you will get the peace and quiet you want.*

Learning to notice and articulate people's probable interests will help you throughout the mediation with all three sides of the mediator skills triangle.

❏ POSITIONS: HERE I STAND

Most people come into mediation with a list of problems and a list of solutions—what they think should happen. Mediators call these initial solutions "positions." Waving a position about can be an effective way to galvanize the other party into dealing seriously with you. *If you don't fire him, I'm quitting. You owe us $6,000 and we're going to court to get it if we have to.*

Taking a position leapfrogs directly from problem to solution. And that solution may or may not address the underlying interests even of the person proposing the solution. Once at the table, however, positions can be a hindrance. Interests—*why* something is a problem and what needs and hopes must be satisfied to reach solid agreement—may be barely audible above the din of demands and rejections. Because the roots of the conflict are not explicitly considered, negotiating a compromise between positions is more likely to produce a limited, unimaginative, and fragile agreement.

❏ MOVING FROM POSITIONS TO INTERESTS

Before people can work on solutions, they need to broaden their understanding of the situation. This foundation for resolving the problem and transforming one's relationship to the conflict is laid during the Uninterrupted Time and the Exchange.

Understanding the other party. They need to understand the other party's point of view (even if they don't agree). They also need a sense of the interests, emotions, limitations, and capabilities of the other side. At its best, this understanding can be a moment of "recognition," a turning-point when the opponent becomes a person.

Understanding oneself. Even more fundamentally, each person needs to be aware of his or her own interests, emotions, limitations, and capabilities.

Reframing the problem. The parties need to shift from presenting their conflict as stories and positions to viewing the situation as a set of specific interests, principles, and mediatable issues.

The next page gives some examples of how the mediator can shift the perspective from positions to interests. Notice that the mediator summarizes the parties' interests without reiterating their positions.

FROM POSITIONS TO INTERESTS

Interpretations and positions the mediator hears: ⇨	How the mediator might summarize the parties' interests:
Pat is asking the company to pay for evening and weekend daycare expenses. She made this a condition of accepting the promotion. The company should not be allowed to renege on its promises. Zach insists that they cannot pay because it is against the company policy of no perks. The VP never made any such promise. If Pat can't hack this promotion, she should go back to her old job.	■ **One side, then the other side's interests:** *As I understand it, Zach, you are pleased with Pat's work, and would like to keep her in this new position. You are concerned about the integrity of the company's "no favors" compensation policy.* *And, Pat, you also want to keep this job, but you need some financial assistance and some scheduling flexibility to handle the daycare situation. And you want to know that this company is treating you fairly.*
Russell says he will resign from the committee unless Walter apologizes for the untrue and nasty comments he made about Russell to key members of the church. Walter counters that Russell is high-handedly excluding him from financial decisions—and botching those decisions besides. Russell *should* resign. Walter says he isn't sorry and he won't apologize till hell freezes over.	■ **Emphasizing common interests:** *You have a common interest in finding the right pastor for your church, and you've worked very hard for a year on this committee. It sounds like both of you would like to see it through.* *There is concern about personal reputation and being appreciated even when opinions differ. And a desire to be included in financial decisions.*
Neighbors demand that a nearby movie theater control the teenaged crowds that gather there. They also want patrons to park at night in the shopping center lot across the street instead of in front of their houses and blocking their driveways. The theater owners say the town should be grateful that they keep the teenagers safely entertained. Unfortunately, they can't control their patrons once they leave the premises. The shopping center charges much higher access fees than the theater can afford. If neighbor harassment of them and their patrons doesn't stop, they will go to court.	■ **Interests as a set of criteria.** *After listening to what matters to you, it seems that a workable agreement has to meet these criteria:* ➤ *The residents need quiet between 10: 30 PM and 7: 30 AM, and access to parking near their houses.* ➤ *The movie theater wants to make sure the number of patrons does not drop.* ➤ *Solutions should preserve the friendly, safe neighborhood feeling—which everyone has agreed is good for the residents **and** the businesses.*

MEDIATABLE ISSUES

❑ ISSUE: AN AREA OF CONTENTION

An issue is an area of contention. For mediation purposes, we limit the term to those matters which are potential topics for negotiation. In defining an issue, the mediators and participants may draw a wide circle: *We are discussing how the park should be regulated.* Or narrow it down: *One issue is kids leaping the fence.*

The mediators combine the parties' concerns and interests into issues. When the parties are finally ready to accept a joint view of the situation, the mediators present a proposed list of issues during Setting the Agenda. This mutally agreed-on agenda outlines a structure for the agreement building process.

❑ FROM BROAD TO BITE-SIZED

List the broad issues to give everyone an overview of the areas that need attention. Later, they can grapple with the specific bite-sized elements of those issues a few at a time.

Issues and their solutions are often interlinked. For this reason you can't always tidy up one subject and move on to the next. The mediator can prevent the discussion from bouncing confusingly from one issue to another by mapping out the connections between topics and keeping lists. Review the specific points (to yourself or aloud) when you shift to a new subject and again as you finalize agreements on that section.

YANG FOODS - DONALD WONG, JANICE WONG
EASTWICK APTS. - BOB THOMAS, MANAGER
(LIVES OFFSITE)

ISSUES

• DELIVERIES
- TRUCKS BLOCK ACCESS
- APT. CARS IN DELIVERY SPACES
- ARE ALL CARS FROM EASTWICK?

✓ PARKING —— • WEEKENDS
- SNOW REMOVAL (SUN.)
✓ NOISE
? VANDALISM
- WHEN OKAY TO USE PARKING LOT?
✓ WHO TO CALL

MEDIATABLE ISSUES

❏ DEFINING AND GROUPING ISSUES

Which issues belong on the Agenda?

➤ **Frequently mentioned.** Which concerns did you hear often or from more than one person? If a point was made during Uninterrupted Time, yet no one has brought it up again in the Exchange, you can probably set it aside.

➤ **Emotional.** Any issue which really matters to someone needs to be included (although you may reword it, or combine it with other concerns).

➤ **Negotiable.** Is it possible to reach a specific agreement about this issue (see next page)? Can you rework it or select a piece of it that *is* negotiable?

➤ **Key to a lasting resolution.** Include any issue you consider vital to building a solid agreement, whether they've emphasized it or not. For example, "How do we handle future problems?" may not be foremost in the participants' minds but is important to sustaining an agreement.

Dividing, combining, and balancing issues

➤ **Bite-sized issues.** Divide complex, highly-charged topics into several smaller issues. In a difficult mediation, list smaller issues separately to increase the chance that they will see themselves making progress.

➤ **Combining.** Instead of listing one issue that is Timothy's concern followed by one issue that is Peter's, try to find cross-cutting categories which encompass the concerns of both sides. If Tim wants to go to bed early and Peter wants to have friends over to party, instead of listing *Sleep* and *Parties*, you might cluster the issues as: *How you spend evening hours* in the apartment.

➤ **Other Perspectives.** For long-stalemated disputes, try joining and labeling issues in a surprising way to help the participants look at the issues in a new light.

➤ **Balance.** As in the final agreement, check that each person's concerns are included and that one party's agenda does not overwhelm the issue list.

MEDIATABLE ISSUES

❑ DOES THIS ISSUE BELONG IN MEDIATION?

TYPES OF NEGOTIABLE ISSUES

■ Behaviors

How people treat each other

Sharing space

Respecting boundaries

Communicating about problems

Noise

Following through on promises and responsibiltilties

The ways people do their work

■ Things, money

Property

Reimbursement

Arranging payments

Repairs

Loans

Maintenance

■ Structure and Systems

How decisions are made

Rules and regulations

Procedures

Schedules

Job responsibilities

Access

THESE CONCERNS CAN BE DISCUSSED, BUT NOT NEGOTIATED

Beliefs	Hurt Feelings
Principles, Values	Perceptions
Child-raising	Management style
Attitudes	Interpretations
Anger	Prejudices
Personal Style	Trust
What happened	Blame, Fault
	Rights

MEDIATABLE ISSUES

ISSUES THAT USUALLY CANNOT BE MEDIATED

Determining the truth of what happened.

Determining fault and punishment.

Addictive behaviors.

Pathological or abusive behaviors.

Wide gap in power between the parties.

Issues where the real decision-maker is not present.

Issues where people who may be affected by a decision or whose cooperation is necessary are not represented.

Issues requiring investigation and disclosure before fair negotiation can take place.

Situations where the parties do not understand the complexities of the issues or their legal options.

❑ DEALING WITH UNMEDIATABLE ISSUES

➤ Feelings, attitudes and other non-negotiable concerns often point towards negotiable issues. Reframe those pieces that can be translated into specific behaviors.

➤ Support expression and discussion of key concerns without trying to get agreement. When they are ready, encourage them to address the things they *can* negotiate.

➤ State that certain topics cannot be resolved, then suggest aspects or related topics you think *can* be negotiated.

Some caution is needed here. Negotiating side issues or aspects of behavior may be pointless when the main issue remains a source of active conflict. And when the main problem is an abusive relationship or large power difference, fair and safe negotiation of side points is probably impossible.

➤ Ask the parties to agree on another place or method to deal with their unmediatable issues.

➤ Postpone the session until all necessary parties agree to attend.

➤ If there's nothing left to mediate, end the session. Consider drawing up a session summary.

REFRAMING THEIR WORDS

❑ FOCUS ON BEHAVIOR AND SYSTEMS

Feelings, style, attitudes, and values may be significant elements of a conflict. Although these non-negotiable concerns cannot be resolved directly, the parties may need to discuss them at length.

Judicious questions can help them reframe these concerns into specific behaviors and systems that can be negotiated:

You said that having her around is too upsetting—are there times when you'd especially like to be left alone?

Terry, you say you feel disrespected. Can you describe specific things you'd like Kisha to do that would be respectful?

You both say that customer service is the key to making this business succeed. Can each of you give a few examples of what good customer service looks like?

❑ USING NEUTRAL LANGUAGE

During Setting the Agenda, the mediator translates emotional, personally-felt concerns into a mutual problem to resolve. This requires neutralizing the partisan language people have been using so that all parties can recognize the issue as theirs.

Finding a neutral phrase that is honest and that is not a euphemism which glosses over the real problem can be a challenge. The trick is *naming* the behaviors, consequences, or subjects at issue without *characterizing* them. Beware also of echoing one party's choice of labels. For instance, in the first example below, you would not want to say: *One issue is the messy office.*

DISPUTANT:	MEDIATOR:
Her desk is a disgraceful mess!	*One issue is how neat the office should be.*
I don't want anyone trespassing on my private property.	*Property boundaries are an issue.*
That policy is sexist.	*We need to talk about how this policy affects women patients.*
We will not cooperate with your underhanded, shoddy business practices.	*You disagree about what to promise customers and how payments should be made.*

ELICITING IDEAS

QUESTIONS TO GET AT SOLUTIONS

What might work for you?

*What can **you** do to help resolve this issue?*

What other things might you try?

What would make this idea more workable for you?

Is there some way we can meet both Jim's need for _____ and Cathy's need for _____?

❏ OPENING UP POSSIBILITIES

Ironically, now that the parties are finally ready to discuss solutions, you may have to slow them down. They may make careless decisions in their desire to hurry up and decide things. Try to channel that burst of energy into generating ideas.

In addition to the questions on the left, here are some techniques to get them thinking about more inventive solutions and to realize that they have options and choices.

➢ **Get a number of suggestions *before* discussing their merits.** Even if a great idea is on the table, ask for more, making sure that all ideas are heard. Everyone may be relieved that they've thought of a workable idea, however, the first solution offered is not always the best one.

➢ **Ask what each one of them can personally offer** that they think the other party might agree to. This is especially useful if all their ideas are about what the other person can do differently.

➢ **Ask for specific information.** Questions about the particulars of the situation can make the problem look less overwhelming, and help people to think specifically and practically about solutions.

Stimulate creative thinking

You want the participants to be imaginative, willing to try something new, less stuck in entrenched perspectives. Here are some ways you can help them be more fluid and adventurous in their thinking:

➢ **The two solution rule:** Ask each party to come up with at least two suggestions, suggestions that they personally could live with. Don't give in when they say they can only think of one!

➢ **Try an unexpected approach**, perhaps with some humor or imaginative element. You want to shake them out of their thinking ruts (which in a conflict can be deeply grooved).

Pretend your boss is on a 4 week trip to Antarctica. What might work if she wasn't around to disapprove?

For a moment let's list all the solutions you know won't work.

➢ **Ask everyone to wear a different hat** for a minute (See Edward DeBono's books for details): an optimist's, a 5-year-old's, a journalist's… How does the issue or proposed solution look now?

RULES FOR BRAINSTORMING

1. No comments, negative or positive, verbal or non-verbal on anyone's suggestion. It is okay to build on someone's idea, or to bounce off it.

2. Don't worry about whether the idea is good or if it will work.

3. Come up with as many ideas as you can.

❑ BRAINSTORMING

One way to spark creative, energetic discussion is a Brainstorm. First, explain the rules (See the sidebar). Assure them that seemingly silly or unworkable ideas will help stimulate their creative thinking and that there will be a serious discussion *after* you are finished brainstorming.

You can brainstorm ideas for solutions to a particular issue. You can brainstorm the criteria or characteristics of a good solution. If you want the parties to feel more optimistic about finding a resolution, try the brainstorm in two columns:

What's working well now?
What are possible improvements?

Facilitation tips

➢ Make a list where everyone can see it. Try to use their wording.

➢ Listen to the idea, repeat it, write it, and say, *Thank you. What other ideas do people have?*

➢ Keep things moving briskly, your tone lively and upbeat.

➢ Continue to solicit ideas even if they seem to have run out of them. Be silently expectant but don't pressure them.

➢ Once you allow commenting, brainstorming is difficult to continue. Respect the "no comments" rule yourself.

➢ Contribute some light-hearted ideas yourself if they are unadventurous in their thinking.

➢ At the end, everyone take a moment to look at the whole list.

ELICITING IDEAS

❑ CAN MEDIATORS SUGGEST SOLUTIONS?

This section is titled "Solving the Problem." What it really should say is "*Helping the Parties* Solve the Problem." That distinction lies at the heart of this FCRP mediation process.

At times an easy way to fix a problem will be glaringly obvious to the mediators. Why not suggest it? After all, they have come to you with a problem and you have the bright idea that will solve it!

This moment is a test of mediator self-control. In the U.S. when someone talks about a problem, the usual response is to toss out immediate solutions: *Have you tried ...?* A mediator's reaction is different, and at first it may feel unnatural, unfriendly, or downright frustrating not to "help" the person with your good advice.

While many mediators, especially those who work with large scale disputes, routinely craft proposed agreements and direct the parties towards particular solutions, we strongly recommend that mediators first develop the practice of holding back their suggestions.

Good reasons for holding back

➢ Holding back means trusting that the parties understand their situation better than you do. Your obvious solution may not be feasible or feel right to them.

➢ If you hand them the solution, you may make them feel stupid, petty, or ungenerous for not having offered it themselves.

➢ As long as you are doing the thinking, they may stop thinking themselves.

➢ If a solution is theirs, they will have more stake in making it work.

➢ Even if you offer a tentative suggestion, the parties may feel uncomfortable saying no to the mediator.

➢ Finally, if the agreement falls apart, whose fault will it be?—the mediator's.

If you do decide to suggest something, offer it in a way they can take or leave, either by presenting it as some other person's idea, or by laying out a number of choices.

I've seen other families solve this by working out a schedule.

There seem to be at least three directions you might take: redoing the morning work schedule, redoing the workroom layout, or changing job responsibilities around.

EXPLORING ALTERNATIVES

❏ EXPLORE THE ALTERNATIVES

In the U.S. we often take a single proposal, then evaluate and improve on it. Try instead to develop several possibilities first, then compare and combine them. This helps disputants move away from position-based, agree / don't agree thinking. It also gives the quieter voices a chance to put their ideas and requests on the table.

If the parties are dismissing all ideas too quickly, ask them to explore which elements of an unworkable idea might be worth keeping. Then for each serious idea, discuss:

> **The kernel to keep.** What are the idea's strong points?

> **The weak points.** Where might this solution fail or cause other problems? When might it be difficult to stick to this agreement?

> **What it resolves.** Does the proposed solution promise to really solve an important issue? Does it meet the interests of each party? What issues and interests does it *not* resolve?

> **Resources needed.** Does the solution require resources or support from other people? Will these probably be forthcoming?

> **Gut feeling.** Does this suggestion "feel right" to them? Can they picture themselves acting in the proposed way?

❏ EXPLORE SPECIFICS, CONSEQUENCES

"WHAT IF" **QUESTIONS**

Let's spin this out for a moment…. What if the impossible happens … then what?

Is there anyone or anything that might derail this agreement?

How do you think _____ (your clients, a judge, your advisor) will view this agreement?

Press for specifics, even if it feels tedious and the participants insist that a general agreement is good enough. (See pages 56-7.) Help them also think through the specific steps they need to take to implement the proposed agreement. Are these realistic, too?

You talk about "being friendly" and also "leaving each other alone." What does that mean on Monday morning at the office?

Jim agrees to fix the roof—how will you both judge whether or not it is sufficiently "fixed"?

Raise the important "what if's." What are the potential problems with the agreement, both short- and long-term? If you think they are still avoiding or denying possible consequences, say so.

I'm worried about this agreement holding up. Expecting kids who live next door to each other not to ever talk just isn't realistic.

I think you really need a fall-back, just in case your boss says no.

Once you have raised the potential difficulties and they still want to draft a vague or unrealistic agreement, that is their choice.

TESTING FOR AGREEMENT

❏ REACHING GENUINE AGREEMENT

Before finalizing the agreement, test whether their consent seems genuine. Do you think they will try to abide by the agreement?

Watch for participants who suddenly seem to be giving in or going against their interests. They may be weary or desperate. You may need to have a Separate Meeting.

Serita, earlier you said it was really important for you to have quiet in the mornings, and yet this proposal isn't going to give you that. Is that honestly okay?

You say Leah's proposal is okay, but I'm not sure what you are agreeing to… Can you put in your own words what you want?

Check: Do the words you wrote say what the parties mean? Read your draft aloud several times during the discussion.

Be alert for hesitations and take them seriously. Some people will finally indicate their discomfort only during the last stages of reaching agreement.

DIFFERENT TYPES OF AGREEMENTS

1. **Changes in the outward environment.** *Revising a schedule, putting up a fence, changing the office layout.*

2. **Specific ongoing behaviors.** Parties agree to behave in a certain way: *finishing lunch by 1 PM, calling when a problem comes up.*

3. **Restoring balance.** *Acknowledging fault, paying for damages, trading favors, stopping a rumor, stating good will.*

4. **Principles.** Agreement about what is important. *Each person will have a say in decisions about setting fees. We want to have more unscheduled family time. We want newcomers to feel welcome in this organization.*

5. **Changes in the relationship.** Parties may want to change how they treat each other. Or they may agree to end a relationship. Even when relationship issues are not explicitly written down, agreements can nurture and give form to that changed mood.

SAMPLE AGREEMENTS

Here are agreements that might have come out of the sample mediation situations in the first section.

Landlord / Tenant

> Parker James agrees that he will look for another apartment and be out by November 30.

> Mrs. DiGiovanni agrees the cat can stay.

> Parker agrees to keep the cat inside the apartment.

> Mrs. DiGiovanni agrees to give Parker a good reference to other landlords or apartment managers.

> Parker and Mrs. DiGiovanni agree that for the remaining 3 months, they will communicate if there are more problems by leaving notes in the mailbox.

> Mrs. DiGiovanni will ask neighbors to speak directly to Parker.

Organizations

July 19 / Interim Agreement

> Jan G., Katherine C., and Mark J. agree that they will not talk to anyone in the organization about what was discussed today, and will tell people, "We're making progress."

> Jan and Mark agree to be open with each other and with the Board about their differences in philosophy to encourage more open debate within the organization. They also want to talk about the ideas and commitments they *share* for GoodWorks.

> All three agree to be careful about each other's reputations. Specifically they agree to criticize viewpoints, not character.

> Most of the discussion focused on significant disagreements about direction for the organization and what decision-making processes are appropriate. People also aired their strong feelings about various incidents.

> Everyone agreed that the Board needs to give serious attention to mission and strategy, preferably with an outside facilitator. Perhaps an ongoing committee or a retreat? They agreed to meet again August 3 to discuss this further.

SAMPLE AGREEMENTS

Small business

➢ Both Gerry and Tom expressed regret that this situation got out of hand.

➢ Tom agrees that Tom's Toys will pay Gerry $5400 by bank check before the end of this month. (This is $800 lower than the original fee to account for the lights that Tom replaced afterward.)

➢ Gerry agrees that $5400 will constitute full payment for his work In April.

Family

June 13, 1996 at St. Paul's

Present: Henry, Jeanne, Timmy, Danielle, Kurt Jr., Bob
Mediators: Anne Brennan, Carl Davies

➢ Grandaddy agrees that he needs to move to a facility. He wants to have his own room and a place to garden.

➢ Everyone agrees that this should happen by early September. Kurt Jr. and Danielle agree that Grandaddy can stay with them for up to 8 weeks if there is a delay in finding him a place.

➢ Everyone agrees that Timmy should handle the sale of the condo. Timmy agrees to consult with Kurt and Bob about pricing decisions and about accepting the final offer. If they cannot agree, the three brothers agree to meet with the mediators again.

➢ Bob agrees to check with Henrietta about taking the parrot.

➢ Jeanne agrees to see that the condo gets cleaned out.

➢ Each person agrees to put two full days into cleanup, to be negotiated with Jeanne.

➢ Everyone agrees to meet again next week at this same time to talk about Grandaddy's finances and choosing a home.

WHEN NO RESOLUTION IS IN SIGHT

❑ GETTING AT THE TRUTH

■ *The parties seem obsessed with facts and what "really" happened.*

➤ Clarify what the parties want to get out of this mediation session. Express your regret that they will probably never agree on facts about the past. Emphasize their power to determine how things will be from now on.

➤ Agree on how they will determine those disputed facts that affect the terms of the agreement (surveying the property line, getting expert opinions on a child's learning problem, official job descriptions), then have a second session after everyone has done their homework.

➤ If the parties simply cannot shift to a future-focus, be clear what mediation can and cannot do for them.

■ *The disputant is presenting sheaves of evidence. Should I take it?*

Let them show photos, pass documents around. Take a mild interest, but keep your attention on the basics: open discussion, the parties' interests, and good agreements.

■ *The disputant has turned up with a friend, saying she is a witness to prove the other party is lying. If I send her home, they'll both go.*

Talk to the witness privately to determine whether she is actively involved in the dispute. If you think her participation might be helpful, meet privately with the other party. If they do not give permission, or if you think she is not an integral part of the conflict, ask her to leave.

WHEN NO RESOLUTION IS IN SIGHT

❑ LYING

■ *The parties keep accusing each other of lying.*

➢ Acknowledge that feelings are running high and that it is hard to sit there and listen to things they think are lies.

➢ Comment on how people in conflict situations usually have genuinely different, even contradictory, memories of events.

➢ In addition to the points made on the previous page, remind them as mediators you have no way to determine who is lying or not. Impressing the mediators or winning them over is not going to get them a better agreement. Stress again that the mediators neither make decisions nor give opinions to authorities afterward.

➢ Summarize those things that they *do* agree on and ask if they can work just on those elements for a while.

■ *I suspect that one party is lying. Can I let the group reach agreement based on false information?*

➢ Ask yourself whether this possible lie will affect the chances of reconciliation or a fair and sustainable agreement.

➢ In a Separate Meeting explore the person's commitment to the mediation and desire for an agreement that holds. Don't confront them with lying. Say: *I'm confused; can you explain X again? Is there anything I should know that you don't want them to hear?*

❑ HEY, I DON'T HAVE A PROBLEM

■ *Amanda has a litany of complaints, but Dan and Paul, the other people in the office, say it's all news to them—they've never had a problem.*

➢ Speak to the *interests* of the "no problem" employees. Do they mind the complaining, the harassing, the hassle? Are they worried about their reputation? (This conversation may need a Separate Meeting.)

➢ Put into words any interests they all share (giving excellent service, getting off work on time).

➢ Don't try to invent problems for Paul and Dan; maybe in fact they don't have much concern with the situation.

➢ Ask Paul and Dan whether, since it doesn't matter much to them, there is something they can do to make Amanda's life easier.

WHEN NO RESOLUTION IS IN SIGHT

❑ TOO MANY ISSUES

■ *The parties have a dozen incidents and issues to resolve, but I know we won't get them back for another session. What happens here today is probably it.*

➤ Build on common ground, those issues they are most likely to resolve.

➤ Combine issues into several large agenda topics. Even complex disputes usually revolve around a few key themes.

➤ Help the parties to mark the topics they think are most crucial, or at least to pick which ones to work on first.

➤ Tell them what you think is realistic for a two hour session and double-check your assumption that they will not want to meet a second time.

❑ THE GERBIL WHEEL

■ *The parties are going round and round on the same issues, the same accusations. How can we get them off this wheel?*

➤ Invoke the two suggestions rule. *Okay, you've said you would like X. What is your second suggestion? Great. What else?*

➤ Acknowledge the information and emotions they put forth so there is less need for them to repeat themselves.

➤ Be blunt: *You've said that several times and I think everyone understands your point. It is time to move on.*

➤ Ask each of them to restate the other party's views.

➤ Ask them what aspects of the situation are *not* a problem, what interests they have in common. This can shift the mood and broaden the discussion.

➤ In Separate Meetings, make sure they understand the other side's point of view, and press them to think of what they personally can offer in order to improve the situation.

➤ Change tack unexpectedly. Do something which startles. Try brainstorming, taking a break, changing the subject completely, asking them to change chairs.

➤ Reconfigure the way you've combined or presented the issues.

WHEN NO RESOLUTION IS IN SIGHT

❑ DUG INTO THE SAND

■ *What can we do with One-Note-Charlie? It doesn't matter what anyone else says or suggests, he just puts forth exactly the same demand over and over.*

➢ Return to exploring interests. Chances are that Charlie feels that some strong interest of his has either not been heard or not taken into account.

➢ Shift the conversation away from that issue or from searching for a solution. Find some subject for which Charlie does not already have a set answer. If they can get somewhere with the new topic, you can probably return to the first issue later with less trouble.

➢ Take Charlie aside and be direct. *You've been saying the same two sentences for the last hour and it is not getting you anywhere.* Ask what he hopes to accomplish, what the best outcome of the mediation could be. Then discuss with him how he can get there.

➢ Speak to whatever fear, need to maintain face, or desire to control you think may be motivating Charlie to dig in his heels. What does he stand to lose if he agrees to settle? (This may need a Separate Meeting.)

Charlie, are you concerned that if you give an inch on this issue, you'll lose control of how your tenants treat the property?

❑ AT WITS' END?

■ *We're at our wits' end. There seems to be a lot of potential common ground and easy solutions here, yet these parties just won't agree on anything!*

➢ Step back from problem-solving and return to exploring interests.

➢ Challenge them with your observations: *Every time we get close to agreement, you back off. It looks as if you aren't interested in settling this situation yet. What do you want to have happen here today?*

➢ Write up a summary for them of the main issues they discussed and any partial agreements they reached.

➢ Admit it is time to quit.

INFORMAL MEDIATION

Mediating Informally

Processes for Intervening in Conflicts

Formal and Informal Mediator Roles

Should I be the Mediator?

Persuading Them to Mediate

Setting up a Mediation

Family Conflicts

Mediating with Children or Teenagers

Mediating in the Workplace

MEDIATING INFORMALLY

❏ MEDIATING WHEREVER YOU ARE

People negotiate conflicts every day. A supervisor meets with two employees after hours to help them talk out a disagreement. Neighbors set up a meeting with merchants to discuss parking problems. A family decides who will do which chores. A store makes a deal with a customer who has complained about poor service.

When those negotiations are touchy, mediation can be helpful. You can mediate disputes in all kinds of everyday settings even if what you do isn't officially called mediation. Informal mediation can be a "think on your feet" intervention, as when you are on a committee which has reached stalemate around a pressing decision, or when two people you know end up in heated argument. Other situations can take months of acting as go-between before parties even agree to talk.

The mediation process and skills outlined in this book are easy to adapt to these informal situations. Much stays the same: even in an impromptu discussion, you still need to check that each party is willing to talk here, now, and with you as mediator. As informal mediator, you can start with "why we are here," move into Uninterrupted Time, then guide the discussion which follows, protecting people from attack and making sure they are heard. You can call for breaks or suggest separate conversations. Setting the Agenda is still useful, and your problem-solving skills such as summarizing, brainstorming, speaking to interests, and reality checks will be invaluable. At the end you can jot down specific promises, even if there is no agreement to sign.

Informal sessions do differ from the structured format presented in this Handbook in several respects:

➢ The mediator will probably be connected with at least one of the parties, which means confidentiality and impartiality can be critical concerns. Who you are matters.

➢ You may not want to use formal terms such as *mediation*, *disputant*, *Uninterrupted Time*, *confidentiality*, or *Separate Meetings*.

➢ The parties may not want a written agreement.

➢ The mediator may not have a co-mediator.

➢ The setting may be more casual or intimate.

➢ You may have less authority; the parties may take mediation or your intervention less seriously.

PROCESSES FOR INTERVENING IN CONFLICTS

❏ WHAT IS A THIRD PARTY?

A third party is a person or team not directly involved in a dispute who intervenes to resolve a conflict.

These intermediaries can have various relationships to the disputing parties. They can be relative insiders, elders, bureaucrats, or complete outsiders. The amount of coercive or persuasive power they have over the outcome of the dispute also varies: they may have the ability to recommend, to punish, to fire, to decide, to censure; or they may be only advisors or facilitators.

Note that in the types of intervention below, several are not necessarily third party roles. Members of a disputing group may advise, conciliate, facilitate or intervene to cool off hot situations.

Impartiality

Impartial third parties do not represent or favor any persons involved in a dispute, nor do they support one side's perspectives or proposals. Of course third parties also have opinions, biases, and interests. However, even if we can never be neutral about a situation, we can put aside our personal preferences and choose to *act* impartially.

❏ COMMON TERMS FOR THIRD PARTIES

There are many third party roles and processes in interpersonal or organizational conflicts, of which mediation is only one.

Advising. Advisors, therapists, consultants, and counselors provide guidance to one or sometimes several parties to a conflict (e.g., marriage counselor, financial advisor, management consultant). Their focus is more likely to be on the long-term well-being of the client or the organization, rather than on the resolution of a particular conflict. They act as coaches, not as decision-makers; the parties choose how they will handle the conflict.

Advocacy. Advocates take sides in a negotiation.. They litigate, negotiate, or organize on behalf of a group or person.

Arbitration is a formal proceeding in which an impartial third party makes a judgment about fault and hands down decisions which are often legally binding. Arbitrators are usually experts in the subject of the dispute. They have fewer constraints on discussion, evidence, and decisions than the courts.

PROCESSES FOR INTERVENING IN CONFLICTS

Crisis Intervention involves preventing escalation or injury during a hot conflict. Separating the parties, protecting people, cooling people down, quelling rumors, and finding help are common tactics.

Conciliation means getting people to the table. Conciliators bring the parties to the point where they are ready to resolve the conflict. Someone who conciliates may or may not be part of the next step.

Facilitation. Facilitators are in charge of making the process more "facile"—easier. They run meetings and other gatherings, helping the group to discuss, to reach a decision, or accomplish a task.

Fact-finding and Evaluation. Fact-finders, investigators, and evaluators are outsiders who are asked to research the facts of a situation as a basis for making a decision. Often they are also asked to make a recommendation.

Litigation means settling a dispute in court according to law, regulations, and precedents. The focus is on determining legal responsibility, assessing fair damages and punishment, and sometimes prohibiting or compelling future conduct.

Negotiation. The parties or their representatives work out an agreement or contract among themselves.

Mediation. A third party who is not directly involved in the dispute helps disputing parties negotiate an agreement. In FCRP's model, the disputants, not the mediator, decide the terms of this agreement. Mediation tends to focus on future actions and relationships, rather than on past behavior.

Mediation-Arbitration (med-arb) is a form of arbitration where the arbitrator first attempts to mediate and only makes an award if the parties cannot come to agreement.

Ombuds are employees who mediate and advise on behalf of an institution or a particular population. An ombudsperson handles organizational disputes confidentially and is usually separate from line management and the personnel office. Other ombuds advocate for patients, elderly people, students, or other groups who might otherwise have no spokesperson in dealing with institutions.

FORMAL AND INFORMAL MEDIATOR ROLES

Big **M** Mediator	Small **m** mediator
Outsider	Insider
No stake in the outcome	Stake in the outcome
Is not a decision-maker	May be a decision-maker
Trained in mediation	May have had mediation training
Formally accepted by parties	May not be acceptable to all parties
Able to act impartially	Able to act impartially
Seen as impartial	May not be seen as impartial
Formal mediation process	Informal mediating presence
Role is relatively bounded	Role is flexible, multi-sided
Authority and values come from profession	Authority and values come from one's position in the group
May work with an "m" mediator	May work with an official "M" Mediator

SHOULD I BE THE MEDIATOR?

❏ SHOULD I BE THE MEDIATOR?

At times informal mediation is just what is needed—or all that the parties will accept. As an informal mediator, you may have greater leeway in what kinds of relationship you have with the parties. You may decide not to use the term "mediator" at all. Other times they may need an official mediator. To help you determine which mode is appropriate, the previous page contrasts the role of a formal "Big M" mediator with that of an informal "small m" mediator.

Before you agree to mediate, ask yourself:

✓ Why was I asked to step in?

✓ Why do I want to step in?

✓ Would someone else be a better choice? (For political reasons; because the mediator should or should not come from the disputant's community; or because another mediator would have more expertise in the subject of the dispute.)

✓ Can I be impartial? Do I have a stake in the terms of agreement?

✓ Will I be *seen* as impartial?

✓ Are all the parties comfortable with me as mediator? Have they been asked in a way that they can say no?

✓ Is another role more appropriate? (advisor, friend, parent, judge, manager, sounding board…)

✓ What happens if the mediation does not go well?

✓ If I'm getting paid, who is paying and how does that affect impartiality?

Remember that you can ask an outside mediator to team up with you in order to offset perceptions that you are partial to one side.

PERSUADING THEM TO MEDIATE

❏ WHY ARE PEOPLE RELUCTANT TO MEDIATE?

Persuading people to talk directly about aggravating and painful subjects or even to sit in the same room with each other is often a greater challenge than actually mediating a face-to-face discussion. Ideally, each person should enter the mediation with a willing attitude, yet most people don't choose to mediate their disputes without outside pressure to do so. The conciliator therefore walks a thin line between pressuring and encouraging.

Why are people often reluctant to try mediation? Of course there are those who, for whatever good or questionable reasons, want to sustain the current conflict. But many people who want a resolution have doubts about mediation. They may think they will gain more through other avenues. Many people are reluctant to get into an argument or face the anger and hurt feelings of the other party. And speaking bluntly to the other party can rightly seem very risky. There is also a cultural bias in mainstream U.S. society against turning to others for help resolving a conflict; adults are expected to handle these matters directly.

Personality conflicts

In the U.S., one particularly well-worn rug for hiding the dust of conflict is the "personality problem." We tend to analyze problems as the fault of individuals. Attempting to address the situation is seen as pointless because personalities can't be changed.

That woman is sick; she's beyond help.

We just have to put up with it. Sam will never change—he is too (old, young, sensitive, naive, frail, stupid, stubborn…)

We have different styles, that's all. I can't change him.

Do not be dissuaded. At times the most important service you can give people is to put a crack in their sense of hopelessness. People who dislike each other can still discuss specific problems. As mediators, we know that difficult people often turn out to have more flexibility and even goodwill than the frustrated other party recognizes.

PERSUADING THEM TO MEDIATE

❏ PERSUADING THEM TO MEDIATE

1. Listen first

When you take on the delicate role of conciliator, your main task will be to listen carefully until you have a clear idea of what is important to the parties and what might work. Before you recommend mediation make sure you understand the situation. Mediation may not be appropriate. In holding back from giving "quick-fix" advice, you model the ways that mediation may differ from other kinds of intervention the parties have experienced.

2. Explain mediation in familiar terms

In the U.S., the notion of mediating a dispute can seem overly formal. Because many Americans shy away from formality in personal relationships, you may want to present mediation using different language:

If you'd like to sit down and clear the air I'd be happy to help make that happen.

Would you like me to be there when you meet with her?

Let's meet together—somewhere on neutral ground.

Having a third person there might help keep the conversation on track.

3. Walk them through alternatives and consequences

➢ What have they tried already? How has it worked?

➢ What might happen if they do nothing?

➢ What are the worst and best things that might happen if they take action?

➢ What do they want to see happen? How might they get there?

➢ Should you, the persuader, mediate or should you help them find a more impartial mediator?

The goal of mediation is not to turn angry people into friends but to find ways to work or live together with less friction.

Persist in your belief that something can work out.

PERSUADING THEM TO MEDIATE

4. Address their hesitations

➤ No one will force them to do anything. They decide.

➤ The agreement is not carved in stone; they can renegotiate.

➤ Even if they don't reach agreement, they will get a chance to air their problems and get a better picture of the situation.

➤ The other party may indeed not want to talk, but asking does not hurt and it may help.

5. Give them time to think things over

Let them have time to make their own decision. Confronting someone face-to-face can be a big step. Accept their decision to say no.

❏ APPROACHING THE OTHER PARTIES

It is even more difficult to persuade the non-initiating party to mediate, especially if they do not know you or think you are aligned with the initiating party. In addition to all the approaches above:

➤ Be direct and discrete. Reassure them immediately that your conversation is confidential.

I am calling you about the difficulties between you and Thelma Parker. Ms. Parker called our mediation service to see whether we could arrange a meeting with you and her family to talk about the situation. Anything you discuss with me will stay private; I will only tell her yes, you are interested or no, you are not.

To someone you know: I understand things are fairly tense between you and Wilson. He asked me about the possibility of getting together privately to straighten things out. Can you and I have a chat sometime today? This is just between you and me.

➤ Try to get them talking about the situation. Demonstrate by your response that you are sympathetic to their troubles and are not representing or favoring the other party.

➤ Speak to their interests: namely, lessening the aggravation the conflict is causing them.

Before you hang up, Mr. Wright, it sounds like this situation is a major hassle for you. I understand why you'd prefer not to meet with them but can I just tell you what it is we do? Because you may want to try it down the road if the aggravation continues.

SETTING UP A MEDIATION

❑ PREPARING THE DISPUTANTS

Speak to each of the parties ahead of time so that all arrive at the table equally included and prepared for what will happen.

➤ **Review what will happen.** Check that their expectations are somewhat within the realm of reality. Ask what their concerns are.

➤ **Arrange any groundrules**, if needed in advance, such as who will attend, confidentiality, what topics will or won't be discussed.

➤ **Help them prepare for negotiation.** Ask them to think over what is important to them. Is there anything they personally are willing to offer? Recommend they talk with friends or family ahead of time about what they want to say, what they are afraid the other party may say, and how they can respond productively.

➤ **Ask them to bring information** (budgets, surveys, etc.) that might be needed, unless the hostility level is high, in which case they are likely to just bring evidence.

Prepare yourself as well. If you are working solo, talk over potential snags and possible strategies with another mediator.

❑ LOGISTICS

Place. Try to meet on neutral ground, by which we mean a place that no one owns, literally or emotionally; a place that is not where they often have had arguments; a place that is comfortable, private, and allows for noise and space for separate meetings. For work disputes, a quiet corner in a restaurant can work well.

Time. Let them know how long the session will take. If you think the mediation will take longer than two hours or so, mention the possibility of multiple sessions.

Who can come. This is the parties' decision. Urge them to include anyone who will be an important part of any agreement. If someone wants a supporter or advocate there, all parties and the mediators should agree to that person's presence ahead of time.

Food. Try to have something to drink or eat at the table. It makes people feel cared for and gives them something to do when the atmosphere is tense.

FAMILY CONFLICTS

> - *Lately the fights between the Greens' two teenage daughters seem meaner, more serious.*
>
> - *Uncle Jack has asked for yet another loan.*
>
> - *Sonya is tired of driving her children and her elderly parents everywhere.*
>
> - *Brothers Josh and Tim aren't speaking to each other. Tim refuses to come to family events because Josh will be there.*
>
> - *A blended family is arguing heatedly about scheduling Christmas.*
>
> - *When she walked out of her marriage, Kim and her kids moved in with her parents. Issues of housework, money, and childcare are causing tension.*

❏ MEDIATING FAMILY CONFLICTS

Family relationships are complicated, intense, and ongoing. These mediations are rarely easy, yet they can be deeply satisfying. We urge you to work with a second mediator.

Cautions: Do not attempt to mediate divorce or custody issues unless you are *certified* to do so. You will also find many situations that are more appropriate for family therapy than for mediation.

Mediators report that they use mediation skills in their own family conflicts. The most difficult aspect is remaining impartial—and recognizing when you cannot be.

❏ GUIDELINES

Speak to the various family members separately ahead of time to prepare them and yourself for the mediation. (Access can be difficult when children or elders or "black sheep" are involved.) Expect to hold more than one session.

Mediating family disputes requires strong controlling-the-process skills. Supporting skills are also valuable. Family conflicts can touch deep hurts. Do people need space to recompose themselves? Protection? Silence from the mediator so that an emotional moment can become a turning point? Gentleness?

State shared principles and interests

If you are mediating for your own family or people you know, you may want to start with reaffirming shared principles or interests, but only if you are sure there is real agreement about them.

> *I know you each care about what happens to your mother.*
>
> *Can we start with a silent prayer?*
>
> *It's important that every person have a say in this decision.*
>
> *This has been painful for everybody but the fact that everyone has come today shows that we stick together as a family.*

Listening for "news"

Ask everyone to listen for "anything new that you hear." In close relationships tuning out familiar arguments becomes a habit. This strategy encourages listening afresh. Then at some point ask people to report what new things they have heard.

Speaking for oneself

Ask each person to describe

➢ What the other person did / is doing / wants to do.

➢ What the personal consequences are for you.

➢ How you feel about the situation.

If needed, ask that they try not to:

➢ Blame.

➢ Speak for someone else. (*Mom's furious with you, too.*)

➢ Comment on people's characters. (*You're selfish. You always…*)

➢ Speculate about motivations. (*You never did like my boyfriends.*)

You may want to wait until after the Uninterrupted Time to suggest these groundrules. In any case, you will probably need to intervene often to nudge the conversation into a more positive vein: *Janet, let's leave the issue of whose fault it was for a moment. Can you explain what he actually does that bothers you?*

Limit the issues

Every family has a large supply of past hurts and current problems. Limiting the topics open to discussion is *essential*.

➢ Consider the attention span of various family members when you decide how much to tackle at one time.

➢ Try to balance the issues so that you aren't discussing five different "problems with Fred".

➢ Get everyone's input and agreement on the topic limits.

➢ Remember, *this is not family counseling*.

If an off-limits issue persists: Get everyone's agreement to change the agenda, discuss it in a second session, or get agreement about how they might address that issue outside of mediation.

Always hold a separate meeting

Check in with each person separately at least once to hear concerns or information they do not want to mention at the table and issues they need help thinking through. Explore how they can bring up sensitive issues with the other family members, especially if their silent hesitations or secret plans might weaken the agreement.

MEDIATING WITH CHILDREN OR TEENAGERS

❑ CHILDREN AND TEENAGERS IN MEDIATION

Children and teenagers can be quite capable of participating in the mediation process and usually catch on very quickly. In fact they often patch up disagreements faster than their parents do. Don't underestimate their potential to contribute.

Young people can mediate also. In some school and community mediation programs, kids mediate for each other; in other programs, adults and teens pair up to mediate.

Adult mediators / young participants

Young disputants may see the mediator as a teacher, a parent, or a judge, expecting the mediator to say who is at fault and tell them what they have to do.

➤ Keep your language simple and respectful. Now is not the time to try to teach the kids anything.

➤ Be careful not to use the mediation as a tool to press teens to conform to adults' wishes.

➤ Watch out for your own biases—interpreting behavior as rudeness or rebellion, having low expectations of children's ability to participate, telling them how to behave.

➤ Do not try to be someone you're not in an attempt to build rapport.

SOME USEFUL TRANSLATIONS

Uninterrupted Time =
Taking turns
Telling What Happened

Exchange =
Talking it Out

Meeting interests =
Being fair to everybody

Agreement =
What you all promise to do.

❑ MEDIATING ACROSS GENERATIONS

Family conflicts and neighborhood disputes often involve both young people and adults (on the same or opposite side of the table). The regular mediation framework works fine, with a few adaptations:

Make sure the children understand what is happening

If you talk beforehand to the parents, ask to speak with any older children who will be attending the mediation, too.

Make eye contact when you give the Opening Statement or directions to see if they follow you. Direct your attention to both the young participants *and* the adults.

MEDIATING WITH CHILDREN OR TEENAGERS

The five kids were between 7 and 12 years old. They finished their agreement in about 40 minutes and came back into the adults' session.

The parents were still really going at it, till finally one of them noted sheepishly that his daughter was in the corner happily playing with the other couple's daughter and the boys were talking about going to a soccer game.

—Community mediator

Give kids extra time and encouragement to speak

In a mediation with an adult, children and teens can be reluctant to say much. Or well-meaning adults may try to speak for a younger person, especially when they accompany their own children.

Create the time and space for them to talk honestly. *Always* take the time for Separate Meetings. Reassure them that you are not siding with the other adults and that anything they tell you in a Separate Meeting is confidential. Double-check that they truly agree to proposed solutions.

Divide into two parallel sessions

If the dispute involves several families, consider breaking into separate sessions after the Opening Statement: one for kids, one for the adults.

This allows both the parents and the kids to have a more frank discussion. Bring them back together after adult tempers have cooled and the kids have aired things out among themselves. Sometimes it helps to have separate agreements as well.

Absent yourself

Once the ice is broken and young disputants are talking about solutions, it sometimes helps if the adult mediators absent themselves (somewhere they can call you if they need to) or at least withdraw several yards. Ask if they want to talk by themselves for a moment.

Suggest to them what issues they should decide. Elementary school students respond enthusiastically to the suggestion that they pick a "secret place" or a "secret sign" for when they are getting mad at each other again and need to talk things out.

MEDIATING IN THE WORKPLACE

❑ WORKPLACE CONFLICTS

Organizational politics—the struggle for influence, success, resources, security, and respect—flourishes everywhere. Chances are, your mediation skills will prove useful again and again.

Formal mediation, once restricted to management/union negotiations, is gradually gaining wider use in U.S. organizations. Mediators may work in ombuds or Human Resources offices resolving personnel tensions. Others may handle supplier and customer problems. Nevertheless, most workplace disputes continue to be quietly mediated from within by small "m" mediators—managers, mutual friends, supervisors, respected employees—who do not use the term "mediating" for what they see as an ordinary activity.

You may find yourself informally mediating within your organization; you may come into another organization as an outside mediator; or you may offer in-house mediation services as part of your job. For any of these situations, we review here issues to consider ahead of time and some suggestions for adapting the mediation model to a work environment.

❑ ISSUES TO CONSIDER BEFOREHAND

Assessing organizational politics

➤ Reread "Should I be the mediator?" (Page 137).

➤ What political forces (people, systems) are sustaining this conflict? Will mediating this dispute, this particular point of friction, help?

➤ What political forces might support a resolution of this dispute?

➤ Is the possibility of legal action or union involvement influencing people's responses to the dispute? What are the risks or benefits of pursuing legal or grievance procedures?

➤ Find out who is involved and who is affected by the dispute. In consultation with the parties, decide who needs to be present. If you leave someone out, will the ability to make or follow through on an agreement be jeopardized?

➤ If the mediation is between people of different ranks in the organization, how can you help them reach mutual agreements without undermining the manager's authority to make decisions or forcing a junior person to agree with whatever is "proposed"?

MEDIATING IN THE WORKPLACE

Minimizing risk, saving face

In the ideal world, asking a mediator to help with a conflict would be considered a wise, responsible strategy. In organizations where individuals are expected to resolve their own conflicts directly, however, using a mediator can be a political risk. Not only do some managers need to demonstrate that they have everything under control, they may lose authority by participating as an equal in the mediation session with their subordinates. Mediation encourages openness, even vulnerability, Because our competence and personality are constantly evaluated by others around us in the workplace, it often feels unsafe to admit a mistake or to lose emotional control. Creating a safe space for honest discussion is one of the workplace mediator's most important tasks.

Issues to discuss with the parties before the session

➤ **Define your role** and your reasons for mediating explicitly. If you have a stake or some power over the outcome, be clear with the parties under what circumstances you will influence their decisions.

➤ **Your confidentiality.** What confidentiality can you really promise? (Senior people may press you to tell them what's happening.)

➤ **Their confidentiality.** Do the parties need to agree beforehand about confidentiality? Who needs to know that this meeting is happening? Who needs to know the outcome?

➤ **Discussion boundaries.** Decide whether some topics or solutions will be off limits for discussion. Note situations where one party may have greater decision-making power than another and make sure everyone understands that reality.

➤ **Authority.** Talk about who has the authority to implement a potential agreement. Will anyone not present at the meeting have the right to adjust or negate it, and under what circumstances?

MEDIATING IN THE WORKPLACE

❏ USEFUL APPROACHES

Use the standard mediation process presented in this book, setting a tone appropriate to the workplace and the parties. You may want to try these strategies:

➢ **Choose a private location**, preferably off-site, where the parties can talk freely and where employees and clients will not notice them.

➢ **Review any pre-mediation agreements you or they have made** about confidentiality, decision-making, and boundaries.

➢ **Start with common principles and statements of goodwill.**

I know you are both committed to giving the best, most humane health care to our patients that you can.

This has been a good partnership, and our company would like to explore ways to continue that collaboration.

➢ **Reframe evaluative remarks as descriptions of specific behavior.**

What does Sara Jane do specifically that you consider unprofessional?

➢ **Define the situation as a mutual problem to resolve.** The popular concepts of team-building, of designing work as a process, and of treating other employees as (internal) customers may provide a useful framework for building agreement. Try to have them step away from turf protection and focus on how each person can help make the *other* person's job as successful as possible.

➢ **Emphasize areas of agreement and potential cooperation.** Acknowledge their differences, then shift their problem-solving attention to positive actions they can agree upon:

Are there any tasks, however small, where you might be able to work together?

What is going well now, and how can you build on that?

APPENDIX

Procedures

Policies and Letters

Evaluation Forms

Bibliography

National Mediation Organizations

Mediation Training

About Friends Conflict Resolution Programs

PROCEDURES

We include here examples from Community Dispute Settlement Program of Delaware County (Pennsylvania) to help you design your procedures, policies, and forms. Our thanks to CDSP for sharing this information.

❑ BASIC PROCEDURES

The Community Dispute Settlement Program provides mediation as a community service. Cases come from direct inquiries and from referrals by the courts, police, and agencies. The CDSP office sets up mediations by phone and does not usually make site visits. Mediations are arranged at a time and place convenient to the parties.

In preparing for the mediation, volunteer mediators rely on a case summary printout and talking to the intake staff. They fill out evaluations of each other and of the session immediately after the mediation ends.

The staff is responsible for follow-up and for record-keeping. A quality control committee of mediators reviews all evaluation forms and cases.

❑ CASE RECORD CONTENTS

➢ Names, addresses, and phone numbers of all parties.

➢ Names of the mediators.

➢ Signed confidentiality agreement

➢ Log of contacts with the parties, with brief summary of content.

➢ Correspondence with the parties.

➢ Record of actions taken: mediation held / court charges dropped / follow-up or referrals made.

➢ Mediation Session Evaluation form is kept in a separate file.

➢ The agreement, if any.

CASE RECORDS

MEDIATION CASE SUMMARY

Case #>   # People benefiting>

Status >   First contact date>

Case Type >   Mediators >

Referral >   >

Docket # >   Mediation location >

Outcome >   Notify participants >

                           Follow-up >

                           6 month >

                           Date closed >

PARTICIPANTS

Names >   Names >   Names >

Address >   Address >   Addre:

Phone >   Phone >   Phone

LOG OF CONTACTS

> 3/16 J. K. called us. Problems getting
repayment. Referred by Jones. The incide
involved snow shoveling and parking.

> 3/16 sent inquiry letter to G.F.

> 3/18 G. F. called back and suggested we
call W. also. G. says he knows nothing about it.

This case management database has 5 subwindows: Case, Participants, Session, Notes, and Mediators.

Mediators receive a printout of participant information and a paragraph summary of the situation. For confidentiality, most information is deleted when the case is closed.

THE SESSION

Time >   Availability

Place >   Name >

Mediators >   M T W Th F S S
          >   AM / afternoon / evening

Who gets file >   Name >

Location called? >   M T W Th F S S
                           AM / afternoon / evening

Times reconfirmed
with all? >   Other notes >

WHAT TO EXPECT AT YOUR MEDIATION

By agreeing to come to mediation, you have taken an important step toward resolving your dispute. The goal of the mediation is to reach an agreement that all participants find reasonable and in their best interests.

What happens in a mediation session? Each of you will get a chance to talk about your situation without any interruption. Then there will be an open discussion, and the mediators will help you decide what the important issues are. If you reach an agreement, the mediators will write it down and make sure it says what you want it to say. Each party will sign and receive a copy to take home.

How much time will it take? Please set aside two and a half hours for this mediation session. If more time is needed, you and the mediators can schedule another session.

Is this meeting confidential? Yes. The mediators and the Community Dispute Settlement Program will keep confidential everything that you say during the mediation.

At the beginning of the mediation, please sign the enclosed form. It explains that our mediators will not tell anyone, including the courts, what happened in the mediation. It also reminds you that mediators are not lawyers and cannot give you legal advice or judgment.

Who will be there? Two trained mediators will run the session. The staff will discuss with you who will be invited, and who has agreed to attend. The program does not allow lawyers or other representatives to be present.

How much does it cost? Someone from the staff will call you before the mediation to discuss how much you can donate.

If you have any questions, please contact us. We hope this mediation session will help your situation.

MEDIATOR CONFIDENTIALITY POLICY

Community Dispute Settlement Program
OF DELAWARE COUNTY

POLICY ON CONFIDENTIALITY

1) **What do we hold confidential?** The Community Dispute Settlement Program of Delaware County (CDSP) holds confidential all communications, written or oral, which occur prior to, during, or after mediation. This includes:

    a) discussions with disputants or their representatives
    b) information from referral sources
    c) what parties said or did during mediation sessions
    d) the content of any agreements reached
    e) case files.

2) **Non-advocacy, nonjudgmental services.** CDSP arranges mediations and provides mediators. It does not advocate or pass judgment. Staff and mediators' judgments or personal opinions are not included in the parties' records, and are not conveyed to the mediation participants or any other persons or organizations outside CDSP.

3) **Protecting the privacy of the parties.** Parties' names will only be used during the intake process and in discussions with the CDSP staff and the co-mediators. Mediators and staff will describe the dispute and the session to others in a way which does not suggest the identities of the parties.

Mediators will destroy personal notes made during the mediation, and no notes or mediator's evaluation of session forms will be placed in the case file. Personal information recorded in case files will be minimal, and will be confidential.

4) **What CDSP tells referral sources and courts.** CDSP staff and mediators will absolutely not discuss the intake nor the mediation itself with referral sources, courts, police, management, media, or any other persons outside the Community Dispute Settlement Program. The referral source will be told, upon request, only

    a) whether a mediation was held and
    b) whether an agreement was reached.

LIABILITY AND CONFIDENTIALITY AGREEMENT

LIABILITY AND CONFIDENTIALITY AGREEMENT

- I agree to participate in the mediation process.

- I understand that the Community Dispute Settlement Program is not providing me with legal representation or counseling services.

- I understand that the Community Dispute Settlement Program keeps strict confidentiality. Any telephone discussions with the staff before the mediation and any discussions during the mediation itself or during the follow-up will not be used during subsequent proceedings or reported to others.

- I therefore agree not to call the mediators or Community Dispute Settlement Program staff as witnesses in any future proceedings pertaining to this case.

- I understand that all materials contained in the Community Dispute Settlement Program file are confidential and that only copies of the agreement can be released to me.

- I release Community Dispute Settlement Program, its mediators, staff, Board of Directors, and volunteers from any liability concerning this mediation.

(Signatures of each person involved, including the mediators)

This form is signed before the mediation begins.

MEDIATION SESSION EVALUATION

SESSION EVALUATION

Please comment on the sections below, indicating what went well and what could have gone better. CDSP uses this form to see how our mediations are going and for follow-up with disputants.

Did anything unusual happen?

Did the standard process work, and if not, how did you change it?

The agreement:

Separate meetings?

Co-mediating:

What did you learn from this mediation?

Did it raise any significant issues?

Other comments:

MEDIATION SESSION EVALUATION

Session Evaluation, page 2

Did staff provide you with sufficient background information?
Yes ☐   No ☐

Was the mediation folder complete? Yes ☐   No ☐

Any problems with directions, logistics, facilities?

Presence of all necessary and/or unnecessary parties:

Were the mediators prepared and there in time to set up?

Follow-up:

    Does this need follow-up by mediators? Yes ☐   No ☐

    By staff? Yes ☐   No ☐

    If yes, please give details:

Community Dispute Settlement Program
OF DELAWARE COUNTY

MEDIATOR EVALUATION

Section One: Evaluation by Co-mediator

Case #_____   Date_____   Time _____

Mediator _____

Co-mediator_____

To help you give your co-mediator useful feedback, please circle what you have observed. Then swap evaluation forms and fill in your own self-evaluation. After you have talked over your observations, take home a copy of your own evaluation and return the other copy to the office.

Praising, encouraging	Interrupting appropriately
Testing for agreement	Breaking issues into specifics
Setting boundaries	Using voice effectively
Taking charge of the process	Summarizing / Clarifying
Using clear language	Asking necessary questions
Identifying issues	Listening
Giving advice	Using jargon
Inattentiveness	Directing too much
Making judgments	Advocating / counseling
Citing own experience	Cross-examining
Low participation	Rushing disputants to agreement
Questioning during Uninterrupted Time	Balancing participation with co-mediator
Exploring alternatives and consequences	Confronting

Please expand or comment:

I have reviewed these observations with my co-mediator: Yes ☐

Reverse side

Section Two: Self-evaluation

List two or three things you did well:

Other comments on how you mediated:

One thing you want to pay attention to next time:

Where on the mediation triangle did most of your mediating efforts go?

**SUPPORTING
THE PEOPLE**

**CONTROLLING
THE PROCESS**

**SOLVING THE
PROBLEM**

BIBLIOGRAPHY

❏ MEDIATION

Beer, Jennifer E. 1986. *Peacemaking In Your Neighborhood: Reflections on an Experiment in Community Mediation.* New Society Publishers.

Bush, Robert A. and Folger, Joseph. 1994. *The Promise of Mediation: Responding to Conflict Through Empowerment and Recognition.* Jossey-Bass Publishers.

Carpenter, Susan L. 1977. *A Repertoire of Peacemaking Skills.* Consortium on Peace Research, Education and Development.

Carpenter, Susan L. and Kennedy, William. 1988. *Managing Public Disputes: A Practical Guide To Handling Conflict and Reaching Agreement.* Jossey-Bass.

Curle, Adam. 1986. *In the Middle: Non-official Mediation in Violent Situations.* Berg Publishers Limited.

Duffy, Karen Grove; Grosch, James; and Olczak, Paul. 1991. *Community Mediation.* Guilford Press.

Folberg, Jay and Taylor, Alison. 1984. *Mediation: A Comprehensive Guide to Resolving Conflicts Without Litigation.* Jossey-Bass Publishers.

Keltner, John W. 1987. *Mediation: Toward a Civilized System of Dispute Resolution.* Speech Communication Association.

Moore, Christopher W. 1986. *The Mediation Process: Practical Strategies for Resolving Conflict.* Jossey-Bass.

Price, Alice M. et al. 1995 (3rd edition). *Mediation and Facilitation Training Manual: Foundations and Skills for Constructive Conflict Transformation.* Mennonite Conciliation Service.

Slaikeu, Karl. 1995. *When Push Comes to Shove: A Practical Guide to Mediating Disputes.* Jossey-Bass.

Susskind, Lawrence and Cruikshank, Jeffrey. 1987. *Breaking the Impasse: Consensual Approaches to Resolving Public Disputes.* Basic Books.

Weeks, Dudley. 1992. *The Eight Essential Steps to Conflict Resolution.* G.P. Putnam.

Yarbrough, Elaine and Wilmot, William. 1995. *Artful Mediation: Constructive Conflict at Work.* Cairns Publishing.

BIBLIOGRAPHY

❏ FACILITATION & PROBLEM-SOLVING

Butler, C.T. Lawrence. 1995. *On Conflict and Consensus: a handbook on Formal Consensus decisionmaking.* Food Not Bombs Publishing.

De Bono, Edward. 1992. *Serious Creativity: Using the Power of Lateral Thinking to Create New Ideas.* HarperCollins.

Doyle, Michael and Straus, David. 1982. *How To Make Meetings Work: The New Interaction Method.* Jove Publications.

Kaner, Sam et al. 1995. *Facilitator's Guide to Participatory Decision-making.* New Society Publishers.

Mock, Ron. 1988. *The Role Play Book.* Mennonite Conciliation Service.

Schwarz, Roger. 1994. *The Skilled Facilitator: Practical Wisdom for Developing Effective Groups.* Jossey-Bass.

Woodrow, Peter. 1976. *Clearness: Processes For Supporting Individuals And Groups In Decision-Making.* New Society Publishers.

❏ UNDERSTANDING CONFLICT

Arrow, Kenneth J. 1995. *Barriers to Conflict Resolution.* W. W. Norton.

Augsburger, David. 1992. *Conflict Mediation Across Cultures: Pathways and Patterns.* Westminster / John Knox Press.

Augsburger, David. 1980. *Caring Enough to Confront.* G/L Regal Books.

Beale, Lucy and Fields, Rick. 1987. *The Win / Win Way.* Harcourt Brace Jovanovich.

Bolton, Robert. 1979. *People Skills: How to Assert Yourself, Listen to Others and Resolve Conflicts.* Simon and Schuster, NY.

Bridges, William. 1991. *Managing Transitions: Making the Most of Change.* Addison-Wesley Publishing.

Bridges, William. 1991. *Transitions: Making Sense of Life's Changes.* Addison-Wesley Publishing.

Burton, John W. 1990. *Conflict: Resolution and Prevention.* St. Martin's Press.

Burton, John W. and Dukes, Frank. 1990. *Conflict: Readings in Management and Resolution.* St. Martin's Press.

BIBLIOGRAPHY

Canary, Daniel J. and Stafford, Laura. 1994. *Communication and Relational Maintenance*. Academic Press.

Crawley, John. 1995. *Constructive Conflict Management: Managing to Make a Difference.* Nicholas Brealey Publishing.

Crum, Thomas F. 1987. *The Magic of Conflict: Turning a Life of Work into a Life of Art.* Touchstone.

Fisher, Roger and Ury, William. 1981, 2nd edition 1991. *Getting To Yes: Negotiating Agreement Without Giving In.* Penguin Books.

Fisher, Roger. 1994. *Beyond Machiavelli: Tools For Coping With Conflict.* Harvard University Press.

Fisher, Roger and Brown, Scott. 1988. *Getting Together: Building a Relationship that gets to Yes.* Houghton Mifflin.

Hocker, Joyce and Wilmot, William. 1985. *Interpersonal Conflict.* William C. Brown Publishers.

Horn, Sam. 1996. *Tongue Fu!* St. Martin's Press.

Katz, Neil and Lawyer, John. 1985, 1992. *Communication and Conflict Resolution Skills.* Kendall / Hunt.

Kessler, Sheila. 1977. *Creative Conflict Resolution.* Mediation. National Institute for Professional Training.

Lerner, Harriet Goldhor. 1985. *The Dance of Anger: A Women's Guide to Changing the Patterns of Intimate Relationships.* Harper and Row.

Miller, Sherod, et. al. 1981. *Straight Talk.* Rawson and Wade.

Muldoon, Brian. 1993. *The Heart of Conflict.* G. P. Putnam's Sons.

Pietsch, William. V. 1975. *Human Be-ing: How to Have a Creative Relationship Instead of a Power Struggle.* Signet / New American Library.

Tannen, Deborah. 1986. *That's Not What I Meant!: How Conversational Style Makes or Breaks Your Relations With Others.* Morrow Press.

Tannen, Deborah. 1991. *You Just Don't Understand: Women and Men In Conversation.* Ballantine Books.

Tannen, Deborah. 1994. *Talking from Nine to Five: how men and women's conversational styles affect who gets heard, who gets credit, and what gets done at work.* Morrow Press.

Ury, William. 1993. *Getting Past No: Negotiating Your Way for Confrontation to Cooperation.* Bantam Books.

❏ TEACHING CHILDREN

Friends Conflict Resolution Programs. 1995. *School Mediation Trainers' Manual.*

Kreidler, William J. 1994. *Conflict Resolution in the Middle School: A Curriculum and Teaching Guide.* Educators for Social Responsibility.

Loescher, Elizabeth. 1983. *Conflict Management: A Curriculum For Peace.* Cornerstone.

Macbeth, Fiona. 1995. *Playing With Fire: Creative Conflict Resolution For Young Adults.* New Society Publishers.

Schrumpf, Fred. 1991. *Peer Mediation: Conflict Resolution in Schools.* Research Press.

❏ NEWSLETTERS & JOURNALS

Conciliation Quarterly	Mennonite Conciliation Service 21 South 12th Street, Box M Akron, PA 17501
Conflict Resolution Notes	Conflict Resolution Center International, Inc. 2205 East Carson Street Pittsburgh, PA 15203-2107 412-481-5559 412-481-5559 fax
Mediation Monthly: The Newsletter for ADR Professionals	P.O. Box 6161, Rockford, IL 61125
Mediation Quarterly	Jossey-Bass Publishers 433 California Street San Francisco, CA 94104
Negotiation Journal	Plenum Press 233 Spring Street, New York, NY 10013

NATIONAL MEDIATION ORGANIZATIONS

ON THE WEB

■ Searching for "mediation" and "dispute resolution" will connect you to the home pages of mediation firms, university programs, non-profit organizations, and professional associations.

■ Check out ConflictNet:

www.igc.org

for Internet accounts, and for up-to-date postings about conflict and peace work. IGC also hosts the web pages of many peace and conflict resolution organizations.

Academy of Family Mediators

National membership organization for divorce mediators, with local chapters. Annual conference.

4 Militia Drive
Lexington, MA 02173
617-674-2663
617-674-2690 fax
afmoffice@igc.apc.org
home page at www.igc.org

Alternatives to Violence Project (AVP)

Education in conflict resolution, focus on prisons.

P.O. Box 300431
Houston, TX 77230-0431
713-747-9999, phone and fax:
Several local websites

American Arbitration Association

Membership organization.

1730 Rhode Island, NW
Suite 512
Washington, DC 20036
202-331-7073
www.adr.org

American Bar Association Section on Dispute Resolution

Clearinghouse for dispute resolution and law. Periodic conferences and publications.

740 15th Street, NW
Washington, DC 20005-1009
202-662-1680
202-662-1032 fax
www.abanet.org

Children's Creative Response to Conflict

Conflict resolution programs for children, schools.

PO Box 271
Nyack, NY 10960
914-358-4601

Consortium on Peace, Research, Education, and Development (COPRED)

The association for academics who specialize in peace research and education. Journal.

George Mason University
4103 Chainbridge Road #315
Fairfax, VA 22030
703-273-4485
home page on www.igc.org

National Association for Community Mediation (NAFCM)

Membership Organization. Supports community programs.

1726 M Street, NW
#500
Washington, DC 20036-4502
202-467-6226
202-466-4769 fax
nascm@igc.apc.org
home page on www.igc.org

© 1997 Friends Conflict Resolution Programs

NATIONAL MEDIATION ORGANIZATIONS

National Association for Mediation in Education (NAME) *Membership organization and clearinghouse for school-based programs. Annual conference, publications, directory.*	1726 M Street, NW #500 Washington, DC 20036 202-466-4764 202-466-4769 fax
National Conference on Peacemaking and Conflict Resolution (NCPCR) *Puts on a major conference every other year in late spring.*	George Mason University 4400 University Drive Fairfax, VA 22030-4444 703-934-5140 703-934-5142 fax web.gmu.edu/departments/NCPCR
National Institute for Dispute Resolution (NIDR) *Research, publication, and funding. Initiates and helps develop new programs.*	1726 M Street, NW #500 Washington, DC 20036 202-466-4764 202-466-4769 fax www.ncl.org
Society of Professionals in Dispute Resolution (SPIDR) *Membership organization with local chapters across the country. Annual conference, directory, publications.*	815 15th Street, NW Suite 530 Washington, DC 20005-220 202-783-7277 202-783-7281 fax spidr@spidr.org home page on www.igc.org
Victim-Offender Mediation Association (VOMA) Supports victim offender mediation programs worldwide.	c/o St. Vincent de Paul Center for Community Reconciliation 777 South Main Street Suite 200 Orange, CA 92668 714-836-8100 714-836-8585 fax home page on www.igc.org other local websites also.

MEDIATION TRAINING

❏ LEARNING TO MEDIATE

Even if you only use mediation in informal settings without calling yourself a mediator, a course in mediation can be eye-opening.

As we hope this handbook has shown, mediating well requires an array of skills in facilitation, giving good attention, and problem-solving, as well as knowledge of the mediation process and the judgment which comes with hands-on experience.

The skills and approaches involved may differ significantly from how you have learned to handle conflicts in your own community, family, and in your professional training. Participants often come away from a training course surprised at how much they learned about intervening in conflicts and about themselves.

❏ FINDING A GOOD TRAINING PROGRAM

Choose an approach and a structure that suit you. Mediation trainings can be quite divergent in philosophy and in the type of mediation format they teach. Some elements to look for:

➢ **Practice.** You should mediate in at least 3 practice mediations, as well as in shorter scenarios designed to hone particular skills. In addition, you should be a disputant in 2 or 3 roleplays. (You can learn about a lot about mediation and conflict playing these roles.) The course should also have exercises which focus on practicing particular skills or segments of the mediation.

➢ **Personal feedback** from trainers or experienced mediators each time you practice mediating. Comment from participants is not enough.

➢ **Well-organized training schedule.** There is so much material to cover! Choose training which has a variety of topics and activities, uses hands-on methods (rather than predominately relying on presentations) and a reputation for covering ground.

➢ **At least 24 hours** of training, if your intent is full certification, with group size limited to 30 (preferably fewer). In the U.S., many states now specify a minimum number of training hours before you can practice as a mediator.

➢ **An opportunity to see several experienced mediators' styles in action,** whether by watching videotapes or by having a training team (instead of a solo trainer) or mediator-coaches for roleplays.

FRIENDS CONFLICT RESOLUTION PROGRAMS

WHAT WE OFFER

- **Basic mediation training**: Open enrollment courses, as well as custom-designed training for programs and organizations

- **School peer mediation training**

- **Workshops** in conflict resolution and mediation

- **Presentations**

- **Mediation, facilitation, and other conflict resolution services**

- **Meetings for Understanding**: a worship-based approach to conflict

- **Consulting** for school peer mediation, non-profit organizations, and community mediation programs.

Please call us
215-241-7029

❏ ABOUT FRIENDS CONFLICT RESOLUTION PROGRAMS

Friends Conflict Resolution Programs seeks to develop creative and peaceful processes for resolving conflicts in Quaker and other communities. It is a program of the Philadelphia Yearly Meeting of the Religious Society of Friends (Quakers).

The early years…

One of the longest-running mediation programs in the United States, FCRP developed a process for mediating community disputes and started the Community Dispute Settlement Program of Delaware County. In those days the FCRP was known as Friends Suburban Project, then as Friends Mediation Service. The book *Peacemaking in Your Neighborhood: reflections on an experiment in community mediation* (New Society Publishers, 1986) tells the story of this decade of work.

… and today

Today FCRP teaches conflict resolution to young people and helps schools set up peer mediation programs. We provide services to anyone who wants a Quaker mediator and offer conflict resolution services and training to health care and elder care organizations. FCRP is particularly known for its high-quality mediation training.

FCRP works in a variety of community and non-profit settings: schools, low-income housing, religious organizations, colleges, social service agencies. Several of our active members have become professional mediators handling environmental, public policy, multi-party, organizational and workplace conflicts.

Publications

Two publications are available from FCRP:

➢ *The Mediator's Handbook*, designed to provide a thorough and practical reference for all mediators

➢ *The School Mediation Trainers' Manual,* which contains a model agenda and support materials for training in schools.